DEPRESSION AND EXPRESSIVE BEHAVIOR

DEPRESSION AND EXPRESSIVE BEHAVIOR

Edited by

Jack D. Maser

National Institute of Mental Health

Routledge
Taylor & Francis Group
New York London

Routledge is an imprint of the
Taylor & Francis Group, an informa business

First Published by Lawrence Erlbaum Associates, Inc., Publishers
10 Industrial Avenue
Mahwah, New Jersey 07430

Transferred to digital printing 2010 by Routledge

Routledge
Taylor and Francis Group
270 Madison Avenue
New York, NY 10016

Routledge
Taylor and Francis Group
2 Park Square
Milton Park, Abingdon
Oxon OX14 4RN

The opinions expressed here are those of the authors and do not necessarily represent the positions of the National Institute of Mental Health.

Lawrence Erlbaum Associates, Inc., Publishers
365 Broadway
Hillsdale, New Jersey 07642

Library of Congress Cataloging-in-Publication Data

Depression and expressive behavior.

Bibliography: p.
Includes indexes.
1. Depression, Mental—Diagnosis. 2. Expression.
3. Behavioral assessment. I. Maser, Jack D.

RC537.D4274 1987 616.85'27 86-29046
ISBN 0-89859-999-7

10 9 8 7 6 5 4 3 2

Contents

List of Contributors

Mary C. Blehar, Ph.D. *Head, Clinical and Biological Studies of Affective Disorders Program, Affective and Anxiety Disorders Research Branch, 5600 Fishers Lane, Room 10C-24, Rockville, MD 20857*

Allen T. Dittmann, Ph.D. *10709 Clermont Avenue, Garrett Park, MD 20896*

Paul Ekman, Ph.D. *Human Interaction Laboratory, Langley Porter Neuropsychiatric Institute, 401 Parnassus Avenue, San Francisco, CA 94143*

Alan Fridlund, Ph.D. *Department of Psychology, University of Pennsylvania, 381-15 Walnut Street, Philadelphia, PA 19104*

Robert M. A. Hirschfeld, M.D. *Chief, Affective and Anxiety Disorders Research Branch, National Institute of Mental Health, 5600 Fishers Lane, Room 10C-24, Rockville, MD 20857*

David J. Kupfer, M.D. *Western Psychiatric Institute and Clinic, University of Pittsburgh, 2811 O'Hara Street, Pittsburgh, PA 15213*

Jack D. Maser, Ph.D. *Assistant Chief, Affective and Anxiety Disorders Research Branch, National Institute of Mental Health, 5600 Fishers Lane, Room 10C-24, Rockville, MD 20857*

Robert Miller, Ph.D. *(deceased)*

Klaus R. Scherer, Ph.D. *Section de Psychologie, Faculté de Psychologie et des Sciences de l'Education, Université de Genève, 24, rue Général-Dufour, 1211 Genève 4, SWITZERLAND*

Aron W. Siegman, Ph.D. *Department of Psychology, University of Maryland Baltimore County, Catonsville, MD 21228*

Preface

Robert M. A. Hirschfeld, M.D.

Reliance solely on the clinical interview to assess psychiatric problems sharply contrasts with other medical fields. Neurologists routinely employ electromyography to measure the extent and nature of muscular dysfunction. Cardiologists use cardiac catheterization to confirm abnormalities in heart valve functioning. Internists call for upper gastrointestinal series to follow up an impression of peptic ulcer disease. The clinical interview is an indispensible first step in a comprehensive general medical evaluation; in psychiatry and clinical psychology it is too frequently the only step in the evaluation. This situation has been changing and will continue to do so in the foreseeable future.

Advances in our understanding and treatment of mental disorders have forced these changes over the past three decades. The efficacious treatments that have been developed have paralleled discoveries of alterations in neuroendocrine, psychophysiologic, and other functioning. These treatments and biological dysfunctions have not been generic to all psychiatric disorders, but rather, have been associated with particular mental disorders. Therefore, differentiation of mental disorders has become critical both for clinical and scientific reasons.

These reasons have strengthened a need for more comprehensive, reliable, and accurate methods of diagnostic assessment. In response, the National Institute of Mental Health has supported research and development of diagnostic criteria and assessment tools. The Research Diagnostic Criteria (RDC), the most widely used research tool for diagnosis, has resulted from this support. Moreover, development of *The Diagnostic and Statistical Manual* (DSM-III), the standard for clinical practice, by the American Psychiatric Association, followed several years later. Explicit inclusion and exclusion criteria using operationalized definitions for clinical variables are the foundations of these major diagnostic systems.

Among the various 20 psychiatric disorders in DSM-III, the criteria for depression have been accepted generally, although certain specific issues are still being debated. These diagnostic criteria have been used both in research and in clinical practice. In the revised DSM-III (DSM-III-R), the affective disorders were among the least changed categories, a situation that is based on the relative satisfaction of the manual's users.

Structured and semistructured clinical interviews have become the standard in research for determining the presence or absence of these criteria. Structured interviews are a valuable tool for accurate assessment of a patient's problems, but these interviews are subject to distortion and misrepresentation (e.g., the patient can lie or cover up important details). For these and other reasons, information gathering techniques are needed to bolster the precision of the assessment. Most obvious of these techniques is the direct measurement of behavior.

Augmenting the clinical interview in the evaluation of psychiatric patients by direct behavioral assessment was the topic of a recently held workshop sponsored by the National Institute of Mental Health (NIMH). The question specifically addressed was whether the clinical phenomenology necessary for the diagnosis of mental disorders can be assessed in ways more objective and accurate than routine clinical observation. This volume results from papers presented and discussed at that workshop.[1]

[1]Participants were: Murray Alpert, Ph.D.; Allen T. Dittmann, Ph.D.; Paul Ekman, Ph.D.; Stanley Feldstein, Ph.D.; Alan J. Fridlund, Ph.D.; Robert M.A. Hirschfeld, M.D.; Marika Kovacs, Ph.D.; David J. Kupfer, M.D.; Peter M. Lewinsohn, Ph.D.; Jack D. Maser, Ph.D.; William T. McKinney, M.D.; Rosemery O. Nelson, Ph.D.; Lynn P. Rehm, Ph.D.; Klaus R. Scherer, Ph.D.; Aron Siegman, Ph.D.; A. Hussain Tuma, Ph.D.

DEPRESSION AND EXPRESSIVE BEHAVIOR

BEHAVIORAL ASSESSMENT IN DEPRESSION

David J. Kupfer
Western Psychiatric Institute & Clinic
University of Pittsburgh

Jack D. Maser and Mary C. Blehar
Affective and Anxiety Disorders Research Branch
National Institute of Mental Health

Robert Miller
Western Psychiatric Institute & Clinic
University of Pittsburgh

INTRODUCTION

It is curious that one of the more neglected research areas in psychiatry is the study of behavior. This neglect is all the more noteworthy because the most immediate and salient reason for psychiatric evaluation is an overt change in behavior observed by family, friends, and coworkers. A patient may be described as hostile, withdrawn, confused, "slowed down," or unresponsive; yet the exact facial, vocal, or bodily signs on which these characterizations are based are unspecified. While many clinicians might be satisfied with such an intuitive approach, we argue that behavioral assessment may aid both clinical decision-making and clinical research by improving diagnostic precision, estimating a patient's strengths as well as weaknesses, predicting relapse, and providing a baseline for behavioral change in general and outcome of treatment in particular.

As used here, the term *behavioral assessment* refers to a broad spectrum of measures that assess directly three domains of behavior: psychophysiological, verbal/cognitive, and motoric.[1] Thought of in this way, behavior is a broad reflection of central nervous system function, and if one assumes that mental disorder involves organic or functional impairment of neural mechanisms, it

[1]We recognize that behavioral assessment has a more restricted meaning to behaviorists. Behavior therapists, for example, include a notion of functional interaction with one's environment when they assess behavior (see Nelson & Hayes, 1981). While the concept of a functional relationship with one's environment can be abstracted from the chapters in this monograph, and few if any of the writers would claim to ignore environmental interactions, it is seldom the focus of interest for these writers.

follows that direct evaluation of behavior should be employed in the diagnosis and treatment of psychiatric problems. Nonetheless, clinical interview procedures do not typically utilize any direct measures of nervous system function. Reports of the patient's behavior, either by self-report or from significant others, may be filtered through screens of imprecise or distorted recollection, censorship, hidden motives, and other protective strategies that obscure clinicians' perceptions. Measurement of actual behavior in carefully controlled situations is less liable to management, deceit, or censorship by the patient and, hence, should afford a more objective picture of the patient's condition and progress.

The approach taken here is limited to the depressive disorders because the authors of the following chapters have begun to apply their techniques to those syndromes. However, affective changes pervade many types of psychopathology and are not limited to depression. For example, Alpert (1982) studied schizophrenics with flat and nonflat affect, as reflected in oscillographic recordings of their speech.

The methods to be described focus on more precise measurement of facial expression, gross body movement, vocalization, and speech pacing. Normative data in these areas are increasingly available, and we encourage clinical researchers to broaden the scope to psychopathological samples, particularly depressed individuals. Furthermore, the technology required to record and analyze facial expression, speech and vocalization, and body movement will soon require only the ownership of a personal computer. What follows is a brief summary of recent trends in assessment, some clinical situations in which behavioral assessments might prove useful, a discussion of depression, and some diagnostic issues that we believe behavioral assessment may help clarify.

TRENDS IN ASSESSMENT

Standardized Clinical Interviews

When a patient meets the clinician, it is usually in the context of a clinical interview. The clinician notes the patient's motor behavior, tone of voice, and facial demeanor to determine the diagnosis. The ability to sense and detect behavioral cues, weigh them on the balance of prior clinical training and experience, and place them in context with other diagnostic information is the art of the clinician. Only crude estimates of actual behavior, for example, the mental status examination, are part of the standard diagnostic interview.

In response to the need for increased diagnostic precision, the field of psychiatry has developed a series of new diagnostic schema and interview schedules that probe for critical signs and symptoms thought to discriminate between disorders. The Schedule for Affective Disorders and Schizophrenia (SADS), (Endicott & Spitzer, 1978) is a standardized interview that collects the necessary information allowing a clinician to make a reliable diagnosis. The SADS has several forms, making it useful for differential diagnosis and change of diagnosis over time. It is also possible to extract from the SADS, Hamilton Depression Rating Scale scores for both the past week and "worst during episode" (Endicott & Nee, 1981).

The SADS, Research Diagnostic Criteria (RDC), (Spitzer, Endicott, & Robins, 1977), and currently DSM-III (Diagnostic and Statistical Manual, 3rd Revision, American Psychiatric Association, 1980), represent continuing efforts to improve the differential diagnosis of the psychiatric disorders.

The RDC described by Spitzer et al. (1977, 1978) categorized more than a dozen forms of depression. Many of these may be seen in Table 1.1, which presents in outline form many of the major categories, subcategories, and brief definitions. Table 1.2 describes the specific diagnostic criteria for Major Depressive Disorder (MDD).

The DSM-III is, at this writing, in the process of being revised (DSM-III-R). The criteria used in both the third edition and in the revised third edition are clearly derived from the RDC, but in no case are there referents to the range of normal behavior. The clinician must rely on training and personal experience in judging whether or not a patient meets a given criterion.

There is no reason that even more precise and quantitative measures of crucial dimensions of behavior cannot be developed and used by clinical investigators. Quantifiable methods for testing various aspects of memory function, motoric behavior, paralinguistics of speech, nonverbal interactive behaviors, and role performances are well developed and could be implemented in psychiatric research and practice with minor adaptations.

Rating Scales

Another means of assessing depression relies on rating scales and self-report measures. Sartorius and Ban (1986) have recently brought together descriptions of the most frequently used instruments in the United States, Eastern and Western Europe, Africa, and England. While many symptoms are rated for their presence and severity, none are measured directly. For example, the 90-item Hopkins Symptom Checklist asks how much the patient is bothered by:

1. avoiding certain things, places, or activities because they are frightening
2. sleep that is restless or disturbed
3. temper outbursts
4. having to do things very slowly to ensure correctness.

The patient then circles the degree to which he or she is bothered by the item. The examples given here (avoidance, sleep, outbursts of temper, and speed of

TABLE 1.1
Research Diagnostic Criteria (RDC) for the Affective Disorders

Category	*Definition*
A. Depressive Syndrome Superimposed on Residual Schizophrenia	Designed for those patients who meet the criteria for residual schizophrenia and have a superimposed depressive syndrome without any activation of the schizophrenic features. (Frequently designated as a subtype of "Secondary Affective Disorder" or a form of Schizoaffective Disorder.)
B. Manic Disorder	Characterized by predominantly elevated, expansive, or irritable mood, but not schizophrenia.
C. Hypomania	Describes nonpsychotic manic-like episodes that do not meet the criteria for Manic Disorder.
D. Bipolar Depression with Mania (Bipolar I)	Subject must meet the criteria for mania and a depressive disorder (major, minor or intermittent).
E. Bipolar Depression Hypomania (Bipolar II)	Designed for patients who have met the criteria for both hypomanic disorder and a depressive disorder, but have never met the criteria for Manic Disorder.
F. Major Depressive Disorder (MDD)	See Table 1.2
F1. Primary-Secondary MDD	*Primary:* A period of MDD that was not preceded by any of the specific list of nonaffective disorders. *Secondary:* A period of MDD that was preceded by one of the nonaffective disorders.
F2. Simple MDD	A depressive episode that develops in someone who has shown no significant signs of psychiatric illness in the year preceding this episode, with the exception of major or minor depressive disorder or manic or hypomanic disorder
F3. Recurrent Unipolar Depressive Disorder	Two or more episodes of MDD without a manic, hypomanic, or schizoaffective disorder, manic type.
F4. Psychotic, Incapacitating, and Endogenous MDD	The term "psychotic" is used when the patient reports delusions or hallucinations and shows signs of stupor. The judgment of severe impairment in functioning defines the subcategory of "incapacitating MDD." The term "endogenous" (or endogenomorphic) is reserved for patients showing the constellation of vegetative symptoms regardless of the presence or absence of precipitating events.

(*Continued*)

TABLE 1.1 (*Continued*)

Category	*Definition*
F5. Situational MDD	An MDD develops after an event or a situation that probably contributed to the appearance of the episode at the time. The clinician must consider the amount of stress, the proximity of the events to the illness, and the cumulative effects of the stress.
F6. Agitated and Retarded MDD	Patients who show a disturbance in psychomotor functioning for several days during a MDD episode.
F7. Predominant Mood	Characterized as mainly depressed; mainly depressed interspersed with periods of euphoric mood, mainly anxious, anxious and depressed without either predominating, mainly hostile, mainly apathetic or loss of interest or pleasure, and other mood.
G. Depressive Disorders Not Meeting the Full Criteria for MDD. (There are 12 subcategories; 4 are provided here.)	These are people who are bothered more than most people by depressive mood and associated symptoms, but who fail to meet criteria for MDD.
G1 Minor Depressive Disorder	Nonpsychotic episodes of illness in which the most prominant disturbance is a relatively sustained mood of depression without the full depressive syndrome. It may be chronic or episodic.
G2. Intermittent Depressive Disorder	For at least 2 years these patients have been bothered by depressed mood much of the time; periods of normal mood last from a few hours to a few days. There is no clear onset, but there are brief periods when symptoms are not present. (Corresponds roughly to "depressive character" or "depressive personality" and overlaps with neurotic depression. It is subsumed in DSM-III under Chronic Depressive Disorder.)
G3. Cyclothymic Personality	Includes persons who, since their early 20s have had recurrent periods of depression lasting at least a few days alternating with similar periods of clearly better than normal mood, with or without normal interval periods. The periods must be too numerous to count.
G4. Labile Personality	These individuals have a characteristic pattern of affective lability throughout most of their adult lives. They shift abruptly from normal mood to one or more dysphoric affective states.

TABLE 1.2
Criteria for Major Depressive Disorder*

A. One or more distinct periods with dysphoric mood or pervasive loss of interest or pleasure. The disturbance is characterized by symptoms such as the following: depressed, sad, blue, hopeless, low, down in the dumps, "don't care any more," or irritable. The disturbance must be prominent and relatively persistent but not necessarily the most dominant symptom. It does not include momentary shifts from one dysphoric mood to another dysphoric mood, e.g., anxiety to depression to anger, such as are seen in states of acute psychotic turmoil.

B. At least 5 of the following symptoms are required to have appeared as part of the episode for definite and 4 for probable (for past episodes, because of memory difficulty, one less symptom is required).

1. Poor appetite or weight loss or increased appetite or weight gain.
2. Sleep difficulty or sleeping too much.
3. Loss of energy, fatigability, or tiredness.
4. Psychomotor agitation or retardation (but not merely the subjective feeling of restlessness or being slowed down).
5. Loss of interest or pleasure in usual activities, including social contact or sex. (Do not include if limited to a period when delusional or hallucinating, the loss may or may not be pervasive.)
6. Feeling of self-reproach or excessive or inappropriate guilt. (Either may be delusional.)
7. Complaints or evidence of diminished ability to think or concentrate, such as slowed thinking, or indecisiveness (do not include if associated with marked formal thought disorder).
8. Recurrent thoughts of death or suicide, or any suicidal behavior

C. Duration of dysphoric features of at least one week, beginning with the first noticeable change in the patient's usual condition (definite if it lasted more than two weeks; probable if one to two weeks).

D. Sought or was referred for help from someone during the dysphoric period, took medication, or had impairment in functioning with family, at home, at school, at work, or socially

E. No symptom that suggests schizophrenia (e.g., delusions of being controlled, thought broadcasting, nonaffective hallucinations, auditory hallucinations, definite instances of marked formal thought disorder).

F. Does not meet the criteria for Schizophrenia, Residual Subtype.

*Adapted from Table 2 in Spitzer, Endicott, & Robins (1978).

movement) are behaviors that can be measured directly. Thoughts and emotions are more indirect and hence difficult to assess, but some believe that direct assessment even of these is becoming more realistic.

In summary, DSM-III has increased the replicability of clinical investigations by striving for objectively defined diagnostic criteria. Nevertheless, there are serious weaknesses in the application of these criteria to patients. One weakness is that a criterion is presented, but the limits of normal behavior are not provided for comparison. The diagnostician must rely on personal experience and training to say that some behavior has gone beyond the limit of normality and is pathological. Especially for the purpose of replicability in research, the absence of a baseline or limits placed on the normal range of the symptom or behavior introduces unwanted variance into the data. While behavioral assessment is not likely to replace history taking, rating scales, or the clinical interview, and while standardization of clinical interviews has led to increased reliability, we believe that further increases in diagnostic precision would result from behavioral assessment.

MEASURES OF CHANGE AND BEHAVIORAL ASSESSMENT

Another important use of behavioral assessment can be found in settings in which behavioral changes rule clinical decisions: diagnostic evaluation, quantitative estimates of severity, measuring strengths as well as weaknesses, charting the course of an episode, determining efficacy of treatment, reaching discharge and termination decisions, and predicting relapse by prodromal signs.

Consider the use of behavioral assessment in determining the efficacy of a particular treatment. A serious weakness of present day clinical practice is an inability to measure accurately subtle changes signifying the first stages of improvement or exacerbation of a depressive episode. Availability of differential treatments underscores this weakness. For example, following a low dose trial of a particular pharmacological agent, a patient may be apparently unresponsive. The availablity of instruments to measure subtle changes in state could help the clinician decide whether to increase the dosage if some level of responsiveness is noted or to change the particular treatment.

Nursing staff, social workers, psychologists, and psychiatrists meet together to develop a consensual judgment on the progress and current severity of a patient's condition. The material that is introduced is often anecdotal (another patient may have reported that the target patient swore at and threatened him), indefinite (the patient "looks" brighter), or irrelevant ("He tried to call his girl friend today."). Especially during the early stages of treatment, behavioral changes are so subtle and complex that the staff may not recognize improvement. In order to detect change in severity during the course of illness, tests could be administered serially throughout the entire period to measure the extent and change in psychopathology in a quantitative manner.

Clinicians are much more effective in detecting mental illness than mental health. While level of cognitive and social functioning are important indicators of mental health, they are given relatively short shrift in clinical case reports. Axis V of DSM-III seeks the opinion of the clinician in the area of "adaptive functioning," but in practice this axis is rarely used, and in any case, no direct measure of functioning is required to reach a conclusion.

Moreover, in charting the course of an episode and determining treatment effectiveness, behavioral assessment criteria could be used when concluding that the patient can terminate therapy because he or she is within the normal range of coping, thinking, and interacting socially. Using direct and quantitative methods of assessing behavior, it would be feasible to set empirical limits that would operationally define the boundaries of psychopathology and health, even when these terms are thought of as value judgments by society. When a patient's behavior improves sufficiently to cross that boundary, the clinician can be confident that the subject is in remission.

Another promising use of behavioral assessment methods lies in the possibility that a small inventory of critical behaviors will be identified as prodromal signs of impending relapse or recurrence of psychopathology. Patients are too often seen after symptoms become florid and beyond the stage of preventive intervention. If such behaviors are found to be closely related to relapse, they could be defined in ways that the patient's family and significant others could be trained easily to track them.

Some of the promise of behavioral assessment is already available (Hersen & Bellack, 1981; Nelson, 1981; Nelson & Barlow, 1981; Nelson & Hayes, 1981; Nelson & Maser, in press), but not being used to its potential (Maser, 1984). Other techniques, including much of what is presented in this monograph, require further clinical study. What is certain is that progress in understanding and treating psychiatric disorders depends significantly on efficient, quantitative, and scientifically-based methods for describing diagnosis, course, and treatment strategies. While the clinical interview will not be displaced in the foreseeable future, more objective measures are needed to confirm the growing number of subclusters of disorders identified by clinical researchers.

SUBTYPES OF DEPRESSION AND BEHAVIORAL ASSESSMENT

Behavioral assessment has the promise of providing additional power and precision to discriminate among groups of patients among the depressive disorders. Currently, biological psychiatry is, in large part, concerned with developing laboratory tests to differentiate among depressive subtypes. For instance, there has been considerable interest in the development of tests of hypothalamic-pituitary-adrenal function, as parameters of this system are thought by many to discriminate endogenous from other subtypes of depressive disorder. Two such tests are the dexamethasone suppression test, and the thyroid-releasing hormone challenge. Sleep patterns and their relationship to depressive psychopathology have also been the subject of much interest (Kupfer & Frank, 1984). In addition to possible utility in diagnostic subtyping, these measures may also prove useful in detecting vulnerability for depressive disorder, in predicting response to treatment, and possibly pending relapse. At any rate, they promise to become a major part of the psychiatric armamentarium. Given the relative nonspecificity of the existing biological tests, behavioral assessments may serve in the convergent validation of diagnostic subtypes.

Tables 1.1 and 1.2 provide working definitions of depression and some subtypes of depression, although the official nomenclature is contained in the most recent revision of the DSM-III. There are some issues of controversy in the definition of the clinical syndromes of depression. Controversial issues often arise because definitions of psychiatric disorders are determined by consensus and sanctioned by authoritative individuals and organizations (e.g., the American Psychiatric Association).

Attempts at definition must proceed against the background of a number of issues. Four such issues are as follows:

1. Is depression a point on a continuum from elation to overwhelming sadness, or is it a distinct entity?
2. Can depression be dichotomized as to its cause, so that some forms are induced by biological events inside the person (endogenous) and others by events outside the body (nonendogenous)?
3. Assuming there are at least these two general forms of depression, what signs or symptoms allow the diagnostician to make the distinction? Indicants have been sought in family history, the patient's biochemistry, treatment outcome, premorbid personality factors, and the patient's behavior.
4. Symptoms of depression are often seen along with symptoms of anxiety, somatization, delusions, and nonpsychiatric medical problems (e.g., cancer). Where there is comorbidity, does the nature and course of depression change? What is the best way to measure changes that do occur?

The example of endogenous depression highlights the discrepancy between clinically accepted definitions and definitions in terms of biological and behavioral parameters. Most clinicians believe that the subtype is a meaningful one, yet evidence for its distinctiveness from biological and family studies is sparse and inconsistent. Endogenous depression embodies the notions that this psychopathology arises from within the individual, and much of its etiology can be explained biologically; it is also believed to run in families as an inherited predisposition.

Andreasen and her coworkers (1986) examined familial patterns, hypothesizing that patients with endogenous depression should have higher rates of familial affective illness than those with nonendogenous depression. In comparing the validity of the several definitions of endogenous depression, they used the Newcastle Scale (which embodies the traditional concept described above), the RDC definition (see Table 1.1) and the similar definition found in DSM-III (for melancholia), and a definition of autonomous depression [emphasizing severity of depressed mood and other psychological symptoms] (Nelson & Charney, 1981). However, psychomotor changes are the only vegetative symptoms included. What is most striking in all of these definitions is the singular lack of attention to behavioral assessment.

The Andreasen study did not support the hypothesis that first-degree relatives of patients with endogenous depression have a higher rate of affective disorders. Family rates for all types of affective illness were about the same, regardless of the definition used. The endogenous-nonendogenous distinction was not upheld by a standard method of demonstrating validity—determining whether the disorder tends to run in the family. Of the various methods used to define the patient sample as depressed, 32.5% were called endogenously ill by the Newcastle Scale, 62.2% by the RDC definition, 28.3% by DSM-III, and 43.3% by the autonomous definition. In order of restrictiveness, the RDC accepted the broadest range of patients, whereas the DSM-III was the most exclusive.

Zimmerman, Coryell, Pfohl, and Stangl (1986) compared four definitions of endogenous depression. These definitions were the Newcastle Scale (Carney, Roth, & Garside, 1965; Carney & Sheffield. 1972), the DSM-III (American Psychiatric Association, 1980), criteria specified by Feinberg and Carroll (1982), and the Research Diagnostic Criteria (RDC) as set forth by Spitzer, Endicott, and Robins (1977). Using inpatient samples, some support was found for each of the four definitions, but the Newcastle Scale definition was the one most frequently supported by data coming from family history, life events, personality and personality disorder measures, social support, and psychological factors.

Interestingly, none of these measures (except a possible isolated item) used direct behavioral assessment. One study that did use behavioral assessment evaluated electromyographic activity in 63 depressed women (Greden et al., 1986). Thirty-seven were classified as endogenously depressed according to RDC and 26 as nonendogenously depressed. Normal subjects were found to have a more distinct facial electromyograph, but when imagining happy and sad situations, patients with endogenous depression had significantly greater corrugator muscle activity than those with nonendogenous depression.

FOUR METHODS TO ASSESS DEPRESSION

The clinician intuitively knows that a patient's speech patterns, movements, and facial expressions are a valuable source of information about clinical status. Clinicians train for years, if not a lifetime, to learn to recognize subtleties in expressive behavior that underlie depression and yet differentiate the depressive from other psychopathic patients. In spite of this training, diagnostic reliability is fair at best. In the chapters that follow, four behavioral techniques that can increase reliability among clinicians are described.

The chapter by Alan Dittmann considers body movements as diagnostic cues in affective disorders. This chapter makes a rather convincing argument that despite the problems in recording body movements, such studies are likely to contribute to greater diagnostic accuracy in affective disorders. In an applied research program, Dittmann discusses issues of patient sampling, body movement sampling, methods to detect and record movements, and, most importantly, methods for integrating these results with other diagnostic information. He calls for a series of research studies to refine and enhance our knowledge base.

Chapter 3, by Paul Ekman and Alan Fridlund, is concerned with the assessment of facial expression in major affective disorder. This report deals with the guidelines for assessing facial behavior and reviews various categories of facial actions and expressions in a comprehensive manner. It then focuses on the three interaction formats for obtaining clinical samples of facial activity, gives the methodology for comprehensive facial measurment, and describes general methodological concerns.

The authors have a reasonably firm normative data base and recommend strongly that research now focus on documenting relationships between facial expression, affect, and affective disorder. Such information would not only refine diagnosis, but it would permit clinicians to measure accurately the effects of treatment intervention and changes in clinical condition. Ekman and Fridlund then discuss the need for a comprehensive set of measurements and various types of standardized tasks. They compare the tasks to structured interview formats for assessing and charting the course of depression.

Two chapters focus on the vocal channel of communication. Chapter 4 by Klaus Scherer deals with the vocal assessment of affective disorders. While clinicians are trained to be sensitive to the sound and annunciation of speech, Scherer notes that there has been little effort to document tempo, nonlinguistic elements of communication, and other aspects of vocalization. He describes the vocal parameters that may be most useful for the objective assessment of voice quality, reviews the literature in the area of vocal expression of depression, and proposes a model for future research on vocal assessment of affective disturbance. The author suggests that relationships between affect physiology and voice production could be pursued with respect to the systematic study of the effects of drug medications on vocal quality. It is noted that while such analytic techniques are available only to research teams equipped with sophisticated hardware and computer facilities, software to accompany desktop computers may be available for the practicing clinician in the near future.

Aron Siegman's chapter on the pacing of speech and depression considers the tempo or pacing of speech in depressed individuals, arguing that tempo indices of speech in depressives could serve as objective markers for major affective disorders. The author reviews the available data and suggests that depression is probably associated with high pause times and slow speech rates. However, the application of such techniques as diagnostic markers must be accepted with the caveat that individual differences may result in overlap with the data derived from nondepressed persons. Because significant decreases in pause time and an increase in speech rate occurs with recovery, such techniques may be useful correlates and predictors of clinical response.

APPLICATIONS

While it is possible to examine many symptoms and identify those components that could be subject to behavioral assessment and measurement, we think that it is important to demonstrate the feasibility of the methods described in this book. Tables 1.3 and 1.4 describe a variety of measures taken from the four methods that assess two key diagnostic criteria, psychomotor agitation, and loss of interest.

Table 1.3 presents 13 dependent variables that might be measured when quantifying motor retardation. Latency of movement should increase, while the velocity and decay of movement should decrease; there should be less intensity of movement, decreased variety, and the overall number of movements would decline; acceleration would be slowed; and a depressed person should have an increased frequency of unfelt smiles. Movements will show greater synchrony and decreased expansiveness; they will more often be truncated and show less precision in reaching a target.

One can see in Table 1.4 how the diagnostic criterion, low arousal or loss of interest in things or events that previously brought pleasure, is handled by the four methods. The criterion will be met in general terms through self-report during an interview or on objective psychological tests. Low arousal may also be quantified in speech by decreased accentuation, decreased variablity of pitch and pitch range, decreased initiation of speech, briefer responses, and decreased overall production. Depression can be seen in the face through decreased brow

TABLE 1.3
Measures of Motor Retardation

Increased latency	Decreased onset
Decreased decay	Increased frequency
Decreased intensity	Decreased expanse
Decreased variety	Synchrony present
Decreased velocity	Movement truncation
Slowed acceleration	Decreased precision of reaching target
Increased frequency of unfelt smiles	

TABLE 1.4
Loss of Interest (Low Arousal)

General	Self-Report
Speech	Decreased accentuation Decreased variability of pitch and pitch range. Decreased initiation Briefer responses Decreased production Wide voice type
Face	Decreased brow raise (or upper lid rise in speech) Downward gaze Decreased eye contact Decreased felt smiles
Gross Movement	Decreased speech illustration Decreased gesticulation Head down Fewer activities Slumped posture Briefer responses

raises, downward gaze and decreased eye contact. Depressives are likely to show decreased speech illustration and gesticulations, a downward slant of the head, slumped posture, briefer responses and engage in fewer activities.

Because these measures are no doubt highly intercorrelated, in most cases, persons using the technology will need only select those of interest and/or those one or two that explain most of the variance among the measures. However, the task of data collection, even of all measures resulting from a particular method, will not be time-consuming because computerized technology will provide the information at minimal cost.

CONCLUSIONS

The list of measurements that can be made in the behavioral assessment of depression can be expanded to include: reaction time, cognitive function, aggression, passivity, impulsivity, perseverative (and compulsive) behaviors, persistence in completing dull or difficult tasks, interest in and care of personal appearance (by serial photographs taken over the course of treatment). The chapters in this volume address only one source of the wealth of available data—motoric activity. Perusal of the relevant literature on measuring cognition will, for example, reveal numerous instruments for this purpose.

It must be noted that until adequate normative data are collected from representative samples of age- and sex-matched normal subjects and from persons suffering from other psychiatric disorders, the probability of overinterpreting an individual measure is high. Along with group norms, the clinician would be aided by baseline data from the individual, if these are available. Usually, behavior is not objectively recorded prior to the need for a mental health professional, but the increased use of home video tapes and movies, cassette tapes, and other recording devices might provide an unusual opportunity for idiographic information to be used as baseline data.

Even if normative data are unavailable, the measures taken during intake or within the first several sessions will provide a powerful tool for the subsequent assessment of clinical change. In recent studies of nonverbal behavior in depression, speech patterning and various nonverbal indicators showed considerable improvement over the course of treatment in patients who did respond to medication. Subjects failing to respond to tricyclic antidepressant treatment, however, continued to display abnormal nonverbal behavior.

Many of the important questions concerning behavioral assessment in the affective disorders are not as yet answered. However, there is no doubt that progress in diagnosis will in large measure depend on the development of instruments that permit the clinician to make differential diagnoses, specify severity, describe the course of symptoms, and account for treatment effects quantitatively. The incorporation of reliable and inexpensive behavioral measures is an important step in achieving this goal.

In essence, a data base of objective measures of behavior similar to the objective measures of physiological and neurochemical activity in the affective disorders is lacking. Therefore, one needs to examine what is currently available and what might be available in the near future. To this end, we present four papers that deal with motoric and vocal aspects of behavioral assessment and that have the potential of considerable usefulness in clinical work.

ACKNOWLEDGMENTS

The opinions expressed here are those of the authors and do not necessarily represent the position of the National Institute of Mental Health.

Robert Miller of the University of Pittsburgh is now deceased.

REFERENCES

Alpert, M. (1982). Encoding of feelings in voice. In P. Clayton & J. Barrett (Eds.), *Treatment of depression: Old controversies and new approaches.* New York: Raven Press.

American Psychiatric Association. (1980). *Diagnostic and statistical manual of mental disorders,* 3rd ed. (DSM-III). Washington, D.C.: American Psychiatric Association.

Andreasen, N. C., Scheftner, W., Reich, T., Hirschfeld, R. M. A., Endicott, J., & Keller, M. B. (1986). The validation of the concept of endogenous depression. *Archives of General Psychiatry, 43*, 246–251.

Carney, M. W. P., Roth, M., & Garside, R. F. (1965). The diagnosis of depressive syndromes and the prediction of ECT response. *British Journal of Psychiatry, 111*, 659–674.

Carney, M. W. P., & Sheffield, B. F. (1972). Depression and the Newcastle scales: Their relationship to Hamilton's scale. *British Journal of Psychiatry, 121*, 35–40.

Endicott, J., & Nee, J. (1981). Hamilton Depression Rating Scale extracted from Schedule for Affective Disorders and Schizophrenia and SADS-C. *Archives of General Psychiatry, 38*, 98–103.

Feinberg, M., & Carroll, B. J. (1982). Separation of subtypes of depression using discriminant analysis. *British Journal of Psychiatry, 140*, 384–391.

Greden, J. F., Genero, N., Price, H. L., Feinberg, M., Levine, S. (1986). Facial electromyography in depression. *Archives of General Psychiatry, 43*, 269–274.

Hersen, M., & Bellack, A. S. (Eds.). (1981). *Behavioral assessment: A practical handbook* (2nd ed.). New York: Pergamon Press.

Kupfer, D. J., & Frank, E. (1984). The relationship of EEG sleep to vital depression. *Journal of Affective Disorders, 7*, 249–263.

Maser, J. D. (1984). Behavioral testing of anxiety: Issues, Diagnosis, and Practice. *Journal of Behavioral Assessment, 6*(4), 397–409.

Nelson, J. C., & Charney, D. S. (1981). The symptoms of major depressive illness. *American Journal of Psychiatry, 138*, 1–13.

Nelson, R. O. (1981). Realistic dependent measures for clinical use. *Journal of Consulting and Clinical Psychology, 49*(2), 168–182.

Nelson, R. O., & Barlow, D. H. (1981). Behavioral assessment: Basic strategies and initial procedures. In D. H. Barlow (Ed.), *Behavioral assessment of adult disorders*. New York: The Guilford Press.

Nelson, R. O., & Maser, J. D. (in press). DSM-IV and depression: Potential contributions of behavioral assessment. *Behavioral Assessment*.

Nelson, R. O., & Hayes, S. C. (1981). An overview of behavioral assessment. In M. Hersen & A. S. Bellack (Eds.), *Behavioral assessment: A practical handbook*, 2nd ed. New York: Pergamon Press.

Sartorius, N., & Ban, T. A. (Eds.) (1986). *Assessment of Depression*. New York: Springer-Verlag.

Spitzer, R. L., & Endicott, J. (1979). Schedule for affective disorders and schizophrenia—lifetime version (3rd ed.). New York: Research Assessment and Training Unit, New York State Psychiatric Institute.

Spitzer, R. L., Endicott, J., & Robins, E. (1977). *Research diagnostic criteria for a selected group of functional disorders* (3rd Ed.). New York: Biometrics Research Division, New York State Psychiatric Institute.

Spitzer, R. L., Endicott, J., & Robins, E. (1978). Research diagnostic criteria: Rationale and reliability. *Archives of General Psychiatry, 35*, 773–782.

Zimmerman, M., Coryell, W., Pfohl, B., & Stangl, D. (1986). The validity of four definitions of endogenous depression. II. Clinical, demographic, familial, and psychosocial correlates. *Archives of General Psychiatry, 43*, 234–244.

2 BODY MOVEMENTS AS DIAGNOSTIC CUES IN AFFECTIVE DISORDERS

Allen T. Dittmann
Formerly of the Special Education Program
U.S. Department of Education
and
Laboratory of Psychology
National Institute of Mental Health

The process of arriving at a correct diagnosis in the major affective disorders is greatly aided by the criteria for each category in the DSM-III (American Psychiatric Association, 1980). The key person using these criteria is the diagnostician, whose skill and experience may make the results quite satisfactory. But skills and experiences differ from one diagnostician and diagnostic center to the next, and they also raise the vexing problem of reliability. A patient who is initially admitted to one clinic or hospital, and later is admitted to another one (or even to the same one at a later date) may be diagnosed differently at the two contacts. The treatment implications of the two diagnoses may be very different, and to this extent, the patient's management over the long term will be quite inconsistent with consequent waste of time and resources.

This chapter considers the possibility that patients' body movements may provide cues that would help improve the reliability and validity of assigning patients to diagnostic categories. The chapter focuses on major affective disorders. It reviews research studies on body movements that relate to diagnosis of affective disorders, and, to a lesser extent, training in diagnosis. Some studies of posture (which is not movement *per se*) are included. In addition, visual behavior, commonly called eye contact or gaze direction, will also be covered.

Much of the literature on body movement comes from basic research studies, which are often carried out in a quite rarified atmosphere. Subjects come to a laboratory that may or may not resemble any diagnostician's office and are frequently instructed in some detail how they are to behave during the session. The subjects are usually "normals," having been screened so as to exclude anyone who might be upset by the procedures. The session is almost always recorded, so that the results can be analyzed to answer whatever research questions led to the study. Finally, there is plenty of time to analyze the recordings, in order to answer the research questions adequately.

Many of the techniques developed in these basic research studies have been taken over for applied research in different areas—in the affective disorders, for example. In the case of some techniques, however, application to the diagnostic situation would complicate matters too much, though they might be feasible in some applications to training. Some of the techniques require apparatus, either external to the immediate participants, like video cameras, or internal, like sensors attached to patient or interviewer or both. Some may be unobtrusive if used alone, but frequently many are used until they seem to make the situation too unwieldy for the diagnostic task to be carried out normally. This very unwieldiness may also prove to be an interruption to the diagnostician's attention, which is quite fully called upon by the task of interviewing, a complicated task in its own right.

Thus there are two factors by which the diagnostic situation may be altered, those that change the physical set-up and those that demand extra attention from the interviewer. How much difference these will make, and whether that difference will be compensated by some additional degree of precision from the new techniques, are difficult questions. But the research needed to answer them is hard to design and has not been conducted yet. So I shall be making judgment calls in the rest of this chapter about whether it is worth considering some techniques. These warnings indicate that practical application to the diagnostic situation, and in some cases to the training of diagnosticians, will be the focus of this review and of the recommendations that follow from it.

Research on nonverbal communication began only two decades ago, though some thought and a few studies about the topic appeared before then. There are several topics to be considered: (1) how the movements are to be detected; (2) in what setting or settings; (3) who is to do the detecting; (4) how the movements are to be recorded; and (5) how we are to know that knowledge of movements is indeed helpful to diagnosis. These topics make up the main headings of the chapter, and it will end with an outline for a program of applied research to put what we have learned here into usable form.

TECHNIQUES FOR IDENTIFYING MOVEMENTS

If the investigator is to identify movements, what movements is he or she to consider? Those that are visible? Those that our available methods can detect, whether they are visible or not? If the latter, is the investigator "stuck" with the particular methods he or she happens to have on hand? In any case, what, of all that can be seen or detected by any means, should be called "movements?"

The word *visible* here does not distinguish those movements that are possible to see from those that cannot be seen, but rather, it notes the usual method of identifying the movement: Someone watches the session, either live or on tape, and makes a record of when movements appear (in the case of discrete movements) or when they begin or end (in the case of continuous ones). There are other methods of identifying movements, and some of them get at movements or muscle potentials that would be difficult if not impossible for any observer to see. The muscle potential recordings require electrodes on the skin surface or, in some methods, subcutaneously. I shall exclude these techniques, because few diagnosticians will have time or expertise for them, nor would their use be helpful in training situations, though they may be of interest historically. Sainsbury (1955), for example, used muscle potentials detected from surface electrodes to study stress in experimental sessions. Dittmann & Llewellyn (1969) attached accelerometers to head, hands, and feet to detect movements in those body areas. Both of these methods mean wiring the patient for the session, a fairly elaborate procedure—one that restricts the subject's motility and leaves the diagnostician worrying about whether the apparatus will remain intact during the interview.

In most studies body movements are identified "live" or from recordings on film or videotape. The early recordings of visible body movements used 16mm film; but film and cameras are expensive. Videotape technology that the amateur-to-semiprofessional could work with was developed at about the same time that nonverbal behavior research was burgeoning—the then-new video technology may even have spurred some of this growth. Today, the vast majority of studies of body movement use videotapes as the basic records for research analysis. A single camera usually covers the features of the subject that the research seeks to study. Sometimes both participants in the session must be included, and the investigator uses two cameras, whose outputs are displayed on the two halves of a split video screen.

Other means of measuring amount of motility have also been reported (Kupfer, et al., 1972, 1974), though not as many as might be expected in this age of technology. Here the *amount* of movement over some specified period of time is recorded. It is, in short, a measure of activity level, a favorite dependent variable in animal studies of response to any number of stimuli.

In between the visible and the truly invisible movements are other movements that can only be observed under certain circumstances. These were first identified by Haggard & Isaacs (1966) as Micromomentary Facial Expressions. They were discovered in films of psychotherapeutic interviews when the films were shown at very slow speeds (4 frames per second rather than the standard 24). Expressions lasting from 3 to 5 frames (an 8th to a 5th of a second) could be identified easily at slow speed, but could not be "seen" at normal speed. Expressions lasting about twice this time led viewers to be aware of something different, but they could not say what it was. The events surrounding these expressions were compatible with them—that is, they were not random happenings. I reported a similar phenomenon in a study of conversational behavior in children (Dittmann, 1977): Behaviors that I have called listener responses (head nods and "m-hm"s, by which the listener cues the speaker that he is following what is being said) are rare in children before early adolescence. Still, in a videotape of the session, one can see tiny head movements that appear to be vestigial nods. They occur at the same places in the rhythmical stream of the speaker's speech as do the full-fledged nods of adults, but they probably cannot be "seen" by the speaker. But the question is: Can they be seen? Is there a "something different" that the other person reacts to, even if he has noted it only inexactly? If we take the practical view that what we learn from this review has to be applicable to the diagnostic situation, these micromomentary or vestigial phenomena should be left out, unless some research tells us that we ought to pay attention to them. On the hunch that experienced diagnosticians might be sensitive to these movements, it might be worthwhile to train beginners to see them by showing appropriate segments of film at slow speed, then increasing the speed gradually while running the segment again and again. This method should at least be tried in order to assess its usefulness.

Another factor in determining movements is the difference between discrete and continuous movements. Some investigators have solved this problem by categorizing. Both Ekman & Friesen (1969) and Freedman and his associates (for example, Freedman & Hoffman, 1967) have distinguished those movements that seem to coincide with the rhythm of the speech act itself from those in which the person touches his or her own body, one hand stroking some other part of the body, for example. Following Freedman here (as most research reports on affective disorders do), the former are called speech-related movements, and the latter body-focused movements. The speech-related movements are usually discrete acts with clear beginnings and endings, with a period of no activity after one movement and before the next. Body-focused movements, on the other hand, typically last over an extended period of time, and while they may be repetitive (stroking back and forth, for example), it's hard to identify these repeats as discrete movements in the same sense that the more speech-related movements are. Further, the two may be overlain, one hand engaged in one type of movement and the other hand in the other, or both hands making discrete movements while one leg is swinging rhythmically.

Probably the final answer to the question what is a movement, will come from the results of research and the possibilities of applying it: What physical acts spell a difference between one diagnosis and another, or add to measuring that difference? Those that do add become not simply physical displacements, but body movements with some psychological meaning.

SETTINGS FOR COLLECTING BODY MOVEMENT INFORMATION

In the paragraphs above, almost all the examples of movements have come from diagnostic interviews. These interviews will probably be the most common setting for the work reviewed here, but sometimes other settings will yield useful information as well. A setting of great importance is the hospital ward. Patient records contain a great deal of information from this setting. These records have immediate clinical use in the ongoing treatment of patients, letting the next shift know what has been happening on the ward, and the like. But patient records are not collected for research purposes, and consequently do not have the characteristics of observations in the research literature of developmental or social psychology. Some of those characteristics would contribute to increasing precision of diagnosis, make the information more comparable from one patient to the next, and improve reliability. To achieve these goals, we must introduce some systematic organization into the enterprise. Ward personnel might not be the people to introduce it, but they certainly would be in a position to help.

The kinds of organization we need to introduce include selecting when and where on the ward to observe, what social stimuli, if any, to present and the like. When and where to observe was part of the method developed by the Rauches (M. D. Rauch, 1953; S. S. Rauch, 1953) and used later in the observational studies of the program at NIMH led by Fritz Redl. Raush (1959) wrote about the influence of setting on behaviors. Some settings "pull" certain behaviors, he wrote, and changes over time (in this case with treatment) appear differentially across settings (see also Dittmann & Goodrich, 1961; Raush, Dittmann, & Taylor, 1959). A strictly designed time sampling on hospital wards was carried out in a naturalistic observational study by McGuire and his colleagues (see Fairbanks, et al., 1977; McGuire et al., 1977). They established baseline behaviors of randomly-selected target patients, and used this for comparison with a later period when new staff and patients were present. An example of research records using social stimuli other than the interviewer is given by Rutter (1976), who videotaped conversations both with other patients and also with "psychiatrically normal individuals."

Other settings can be used aside from hospitals. Hinchliffe, Hooper, Roberts, & Vaughn (1975) compared couples (one of whom was a depressed patient) with other couples (one of whom was a surgical patient) noting hand movements and posture from videotapes of the sessions. These nonverbal behaviors, in conjunction with some verbal ones (speed of speech, for instance), differentiated the couples. The motility measures used by Kupfer et al. (1972, 1974), cited above, can be used with telemetric recording while patients are in places other than the interview room. Telemetric recording would be suitable for both inpatients and outpatients, though the technique may be carried out more easily under the relatively controlled conditions of the hospital.

Despite the obvious promise of these studies to give us a glimpse at the behavior of patients outside the interviewer's office, only a few studies can be called upon to show the advantages of this approach, and the publications are likely to be fairly old. The overwhelming majority of studies of patients' body movements are, in fact, studies of the diagnostic interview, video-recorded in the interviewer's office or some simulation of it. This is probably not simply because investigators judge the diagnostic interview to be the ideal place to collect their records, but because inertia has confined them to it. I shall expand on this problem in the last section of the paper.

Personnel to Identify Movements

In the usual diagnostic interview, the diagnostician does everything: following the interview outline (perhaps even writing it), making records of the patient's responses, interpreting the whole record, and finally, arriving at a diagnostic classification. Nonverbal behavior has received more and more attention during the last couple of decades, and diagnostic interviewers, along with psychotherapists and other members of the mental health team, have been urged to pay more attention to these behaviors as adjuncts to the other sources of information they use in their work. Just how interviewers and other professionals are supposed to do this, and indeed whether it is possible to, is the topic of this section.

The question of the diagnostician recording body movements is one of how to budget one's attentional capacity. As Broadbent pointed out, (1958, 1971) there is a limit to how much one can "pay attention" to whatever stimuli impinge on the perceptual system. To say that one cannot attend to two things at once is an incomplete statement, according to Broadbent. What one cannot do is to exceed one's attentional capacity. If two stimuli are of equal intensity and both are simple, they can both be attended to. If one is of more intense or more complicated, then they cannot. Intensity makes common sense, but not complexity. What makes a stimulus complex? It is a matter of the information value of the stimulus. The ones that are densely packed with information get selected and are perceived, that is, get through the attentional filter, to be processed as stimuli.

"Densely packed" is an information theory concept that has to do with coding. I described coding at some length in an earlier paper (Dittmann, 1978, 1972). Language is a highly coded set of stimuli for the listener, and facial expression is, too. Some body movements are parts of agreed-upon codes, just as language is—for example, the movements in American Sign Language. The movements that Ekman and his colleagues have called emblems also exemplify codes (see Johnson, Ekman, & Friesen, 1975). Emblems are movements that have a direct counterpart in words, and are known to a sizeable group, for example the movements that mean "Sit down beside me," or "Be silent, hush!'' or ''Come here.'' But such language-like movements make up a very small proportion of the totality of movements in hearing people. Most movements are not specifically coded, and are thus lower in information density.

The implication of this reasoning is that it is difficult for an interviewer to pay attention to both the ''content'' of the interview, which is language based, and the facial expressions of his patient at the same time, and even more difficult to attend also to body movements. This implication is complicated by the fact that the information density of the content varies from time to time during the interview. Speakers pause, are sometimes silent for a time, so movement information can be attended to. Speech-related movements, the discrete types of movement, are absent at those times, but body-focused movements, the continuous and rhythmical ones, remain. Furthermore, during talking, the information density of the speech in an interview varies considerably from time to time. Patients' stereotyped responses and interviewers' well-rehearsed questions take up less of the interviewer's attentional capacity than talk of new and unexpected material. So the interviewer's ability to pay attention to non-speech events ebbs and flows during the session.

The result of these varying levels of attention is that the interviewer as a source of information about body movement should be considered unreliable at best, and virtually out of the picture much of the time. I have no direct experimental evidence for this in the case of language, but I do have some that bears very closely from a study in the Laboratory of Psychology at the National Institute of Mental Health (Dittmann, Parloff, & Boomer, 1965). The topic was reception of facial information compared with bodily expression. The study was spurred by the common urging of mental-health workers to attend more carefully to body movements in their patients. The stimulus material was a series of 6-second film clips from an interview with a very expressive woman. In some of these the facial and bodily expressions were compatible—smiling face and relaxed body, or face disturbed in one way or another and tense body. In some other stimuli, the two were not compatible, namely smiling face and tense body (we never found the fourth possibility, disturbed face and relaxed body, in this interview).

The study used two groups of subjects: experienced mental health workers (psychiatrists, psychiatric nurses, social workers at Chestnut Lodge), and experienced professional dancers (from a troupe in a visiting musical). The stimulus presentation was first the series of clips shown as whole pictures, then the same series shown again with the face blocked out, then finally the whole picture again. The results were that the mental health workers responded to facial cues only in the first presentation, were astonished in the second (where the face was unavailable) that there was so much going on in the body, and then responded in the third presentation again only to the face. The professional dancers, on the other hand, responded to the face in the first presentation, to the body in the second, but in the third they still attended to the body even though the facial expressions were again visible.

We concluded that without some special training, people pay attention to the face, that the face is commanding in comparison with the body. Mental health workers, in spite of all the enjoiners to broaden their vision, can apparently not get themselves to pay less attention to facial expression when it is available to them on the screen. Professional dancers can, either because they were selectively interested in this type of expression even before chosing a profession, or because their training attuned them to it. In the terms introduced above, facial expression is much higher in information density than bodily expression, such that the former crowds the latter in competition for attention—at least for the mental health workers, who represent the group in which diagnostic interviewers are likely to be found.

As I stated above, this is not direct evidence for the contention that diagnostic interviewers are unreliable observers of all but the "content" of the interview. The situation for interviewers may be different than our study would have us believe, for the judges of expression did not include the interviewer in the series of film clips. Whether he paid attention to the patient's bodily expression at the time of this interview we can never know. But if a perceptual principle is involved, and I believe there is one, it would apply to him, too. The principle is this: There is a hierarchy of stimuli, as far as information density is concerned, from language to facial expression to body movement. If so, we can expect interviewers to pay most attention to the language-related aspects of the interview, then to the facial expressions, and finally to body movement, whenever any attentional capacity is left over. Our study offers evidence only for the relationship between the second and third steps in this hierarchy, and does not include the first, but the implications of the study for the first step are very strong.

Waxer (1974a, 1974b, 1976) appears to have presented some evidence on this first step, by showing that more experienced counselors, counseling faculty and graduate students in counseling, could identify depressed, compared with nondepressed psychiatric patients on the basis of nonverbal cues alone, better than undergraduate psychology students. Experience apparently attuned these counselors to the nonverbal. But they were not the interviewers in the sessions, so their relative attention to the verbal versus the nonverbal was not tested directly.

For all these reasons, it would seem that no one with immediate clinical responsibility for a patient can pay attention to the types of bodily expression that might help clarify the diagnosis of affective disorder in that patient. That would include diagnostic interviewers, nurses, and other ward personnel. Such a restriction, however, is not included in the reasoning given here. The restriction applies only to those who are asked to attend to bodily expression *at the same time* they are responsible for attending to content. The person who serves as interviewer is fully capable of identifying body movements under circumstances where other input is controlled, where speech and perhaps also facial expression are blocked out. So the interviewer and nurse could collect information about body movements in interviews or other situations that are being conducted by someone else.

METHODS FOR RECORDING BODY MOVEMENTS

The text so far has said simply that in research studies on body movements the movements are usually recorded on videotape. That is an exaggeration of the capabilities of videotape, of course: It records everything in view of its lens, not just the movements. A real, live person has to look at the tapes to identify the movements. In some studies, this identification is done in the actual situation, not in the taped recording of it, and in a very few the movements are identified by devices that respond to movement. With the exception of this last (of which more will be said below), then, a person identifies the movements.

A six-decade history of research lies behind this method of making research data out of live (or recorded) events, called by various names, usually observational methodology or naturalistic observation. The first reference is usually to Olson's (1929) dissertation, published as *The Measurement of Nervous Habits in Normal Children*. His work showed that high reliability is possible in making live observations, and that everyday behaviors may yield objective data. Observational methodology has developed to its highest level in studies of children, but certain problems are always present, to be solved in each study. The method could be called more a body of know-how than a body of knowledge.

My list of the problems in live observation is this: (1) how to distill from all of the myriad things that living human beings are constantly doing, those particular activities that the research is to focus upon; (2) how to be sure that the behaviors that do get observed are representative of the subjects' behaviors in general; (3) how to develop some system of recording the behaviors; (4) how to be sure that the observers are not biasing what they are recording; (5) how to be sure that they are not by their very presence influencing the situation and thus the behaviors they hope to be recording; and (6) how to make the whole procedure psychometrically sound, that is, reliable and valid—in short scientifically useful. Other observers of the observation-methodology scene may list these problems in a different order, or have a different list. An excellent discussion may be found in Weick (1968).

1. To decide what particular behaviors to observe, one needs some ideas in advance—a "theory" may be too formal for this stage of research in body movements. Most ideas now come from published studies, work in progress that investigators learn about at meetings, and so on. In the body movement field, there are many leads from the literature. As far as knowing what to observe, it

should be noted that there is a lot to choose from, but the field of body movement is still much more closely defined than that of, say, social interaction in classrooms, where the possibilities are staggeringly large.

2. Deciding which movements are representative may be easy or difficult. If one is to study movements during the diagnostic interview, the problem is not large: One can sample the time randomly during those interviews, or make movement counts for the entire time. Taking observations in other settings, however, is another matter. The point here is that the settings in which observations are made must be comparable from one patient to another and from one time to another if the total information about movement is to be valid.

3. Recording behavior begins with inventing categories within which the behaviors may be tallied, then proceeds with the actual tallying. To do the tallying, the observer isolates from the stream of behavior those acts in which the research is interested, and assigns those acts to the categories that were invented for the project. If the observations are carried out "live," the observer's attention capacity must be taken into account. If assigning acts to this particular set of categories requires very much interpreting or inferring, or if the list of categories is very long, the observer cannot encompass the task, and the results will suffer. It is often amazing how much can be absorbed by an observer, but each set of categories must be checked out in trial runs. When using videotaped records, this problem is alleviated, but not eliminated. The tape can be reviewed over and over in case of doubt, and yet detailed reviewing is very tedious and workers may become careless as time goes on. And tapes do not eliminate the problem of categories that demand interpretation. Most of these may be considered bad categories, ripe for revision.

Sets of categories are almost always invented *ad hoc* for each study, leading to questionable comparability of results across studies. In trying to develop a method of using observations as an adjunct to diagnosis, this will be a problem. The next section will review comparability and disparity of movement categories as specific studies of body movement and affective disorders.

4. The danger of observers introducing bias to their results has been a very lively topic in observational methodology. In the mid-1970s a group of investigators at SUNY Stony Brook published a number of studies about the problems of bias and reliability in observations. A useful summary of this work may be found in Kent and Foster (1977). Briefly, the findings are these: If you deliberately build up strong expectations in naive observers (undergraduate students in most of these studies) about specific categories of behavior, the observations will show bias effects for those particular categories, but not for others. In general, without such strong manipulations, bias is hard to find. These conclusions, however, should not lull us into believing that there is no danger of observer bias. A number of articles in the literature list several common-sense precautions against it: low-inference categories, having observers "blind" to the study's

hypotheses, careful training on standard material (usually on videotape) to achieve predetermined levels of reliability, and the like.

A type of bias called "observer drift" has been mentioned several times in the literature. This is said to result when observers, working over a long period of time, unknowingly alter their criteria for some categories, so that eventually those categories change meaning. Just how often this phenomenon occurs is hard to tell. At least one study that claims to find it, Kent et al. (1974), is unclear when one considers the large number of comparisons and small number of "significant differences." We should be warned, however, that if observer drift does happen, any standardized observation system that might be developed as a diagnostic aid would be precisely where it might be found. Again, precautions are called for.

5. The question of how much the presence of observers alters the behavior of those being observed is a vexing one. In some situations where one might expect an effect, such as home observations (Johnson & Bolstad, 1975), there was none. Similarly, Hagan et al. (1975) found that amount, rate, and nature of staff interactions were unaffected by presence or absence of an observer (data obtained from a concealed microphone). In some others, on the other hand, an effect was evident. Mercatoris & Craighead (1974) found that presence of an observer in a classroom increased teacher-student interactions, but did not affect student behaviors. The possible effects of placing miniature transmitters on subjects for recording speech has been assessed in two studies: Purcell & Brady (1966) and Moos (1968). In the former, adolescent subjects grew accustomed to the devices in a few days. In the latter, very disturbed psychiatric patients showed little difference, the difference being increased purposeful activity. My experience is that subjects and patients usually simply get used to having observers around, but often the investigator gets the feeling that things would be different if there were none. Openness about the purpose of the study, and about the records themselves, and ample time to get acquainted are usually reassuring—but there are no guarantees.

6. The main problems with achieving acceptable psychometric quality in observations is in developing techniques that are reliable and valid. Of these two factors, validity is much harder to conceptualize and measure, so it should come as no surprise that reliability has received the lion's share of attention. High reliabilitites are easy to achieve in observations if precautions are observed that are similar to those for insuring against observer bias: a reasonable task for the observers to grasp without overloading their perceptual capacity, categories that do not require far-reaching inferences to code, training observers so that they are at home with the task. Virtually all observational studies include ways of taking account of these cautions, and they use reliability checks as the measure of success. These checks can also tell when the system is getting to be overloaded. Rosenfeld (1982, pp. 221–224) tested the ability of observers to record move-

ments of three types while watching subjects through a one-way mirror. Their reliability was very high if they confined their observations to one body area (head or hands), but it was unsatisfactory when they tried to observe both at once. In most observational research, reliability checks are repeated throughout the course of the study, and with good reason. Two studies, from different research centers and using different sets of categories (Romanczyk et al., 1973; Reid, 1970), have shown that reliability is high while it is being assessed, and unacceptably low when it is not (but checked covertly). Another problem, uncovered by Guttman et al., (1971), is the effect on reliability of low morale in the observer team. Observing can be a very boring task, and regular meetings and discussions were found to alleviate this problem.

We may conclude that data from observations can be very respectable from both psychological and psychometric points of view. Data from observations are more work to collect than data from rating scales and checklists, but they have the distinct advantage of immediacy: The judgment of presence or absence of a behavior is made on the spot, whether live or from tape. It does not depend on memory of events during an earlier interview or over a whole week. It does not depend, either, on the judge's understanding of some relatively abstract term, like "aggressive" or "depressed." These inferences can be made *after* the data are collected—if the categories for observations are properly low-inference and behavior-oriented. Observational data are also useful later on when other questions are asked, questions that may organize the same data under quite different points of view, and whose answers will make quite different inferences from the original data.

Observations are not the only way to obtain data about body movements. The development of miniaturized electronics has enabled investigators to make remote-recording sensors of movements. Other types of sensors are also possible, to read the general activity level of a person as seated, or as lying in bed. The disadvantages of the techniques developed by Sainsbury (1955), and Dittmann and Llewellyn (1969), which wire the subject to the apparatus and limit spontaneity, are no longer with us. Yet these more modern methods have hardly been used at all in body movement research. Greden & Carroll (1981) reviewed monitoring techniques, and included one reported by Kupfer et al., (1972, 1974). It is a wrist transmitter 2.2 cm in diameter and 6.7 cm long, containing an FM transmitter, developed after Delgado's method for measuring activity level in animals. The FM signal is modulated by movements of a very small steel ball that can move within the coil of the oscillator (for a technical description see Foster et al., 1972). While results of a study of patients with affective disorders show some intriguing possibilities, they are not strong results (see the following section). Still, one would expect that techniques like this would have been explored more thoroughly. Current sensors, working on the same principle, could be made much smaller and even less obtrusive.

A mechanical method for counting movements by a specially reworked wristwatch was developed by Schulman and Reisman (1959) and further developed by Bell (1968). Other methods that might be applied are those related to the stabilimeter (see Lewis & Wilson, 1970), a device long used to measure the activity level of infants. Originally developed to be inserted in cribs for detection of movements as the child changes position, twitches, or whatever, these devices could be used in chairs where patients sit (see Foshee, 1958), in or away from the formal interview, or connected to their beds.

One problem with output from sensors is that the sensor does the coding. That is, it puts out a signal whenever the movement exceeds the threshold for the device. A movement of uncrossing and recrossing the legs for example, could stimulate wrist-mounted sensor; a human coder, on the other hand, seeing this action through a one-way mirror or on a videotape, would not score a hand movement. Apart from such accidental secondary effects, only one body area is measured by a wrist sensor. The original set-up of this device, however, was for a system of six sensors, each with its own FM receiver. Thus any combination of body areas could be measured. Again, the possibilities seem so open that it is very surprising not to see some follow-up on this measurement technique.

RESEARCH FINDINGS ON BODY MOVEMENTS IN AFFECTIVE DISORDERS

Of all psychopathologies, the affective disorders would appear the most appropriate for research in body movement. From a commonsense standpoint, manic patients are active, and depressed patients are slowed down, so the simple amount of movement should tell the difference. As we look at this literature, we find this prediction only partially true. The interesting thing is that there are complications in the interaction terms of some studies that might lead to some greater precision.

In spite of the appropriateness of measuring movements as they relate to affective disorders, the total output of the research is not very large. Also, although one might think that the manic patients would be as appropriate for this type of measurement as the depressed, most of the work has been concerned only with depressed patients. About a third of the studies have used eye contact as the dependent variable, and some of the others have included posture as one of the variables. All studies but three used videotape (Kupfer et al., 1974; Youngren & Lewisohn, 1980; Ranelli & Miller, 1981).

Depressed patients are likely to hold their heads down in interviews, while manics hold theirs high (Fairbanks et al., 1982; Waxer, 1974a). In the depressed, hands engage in tapping (Fairbanks et al., 1982), and in more body-focused movements (described in the first section of this chapter). Steingart & Freedman (1975) found body-focused movements to have more form in depressed patients than they do in schizophrenic patients. Speech-related movements are less frequent in depressed patients than in normals, and the ratio of these movements to the body focused movements is lower (Kiritz, 1973; see also Ekman & Friesen, 1974), even when the amount of verbalization is partialled out. Ulrich & Harms (1979) found a decrease in the body-focused movements and an increase in the speech-related movements with improvement. Freedman (1972) compared 10-minute segments of initial interviews with depressed and paranoid patients on the relative amounts of these two types of movement, and found the speech-related to be about ⅔ as frequent in the depressed patients as they were in the paranoid ones, and the body-focused to be somewhat higher in duration in the depressed (with this small number of observations, Freedman did not feel it appropriate to compute statistical tests on these data). Bouhuys (1984) studied the relationship between these two types of movement in interviews with depressives before treatment and short-term improvement. Typical of those who improve are fewer body-focused and more speech-related movements. One report (Ranelli & Miller, 1981) gives movement data on only some of its depressed patients. They were subjects in a double-blind study of amytriptyline, and results on only those who received the medication were reported. Still, from this reduced sample it is possible to draw some conclusions: Grooming, which is a type of body-focused movement, is higher among the patients than in the group of normals, and head aversion is higher as well. Finally, Jones & Pansa (1979) found more body contact in depressive patients than in schizophrenics (or in the control groups selected for both these kinds of patients). Frequency of these movements was higher, and their duration even more pronounced. Caution is due on interpreting all of these comparisons of body-focused and speech-related movements, because we do not have unanimity on the subject: Youngren & Lewisohn (1980) found no differences, although their patient group was not really in the major affective disorder range, and their measure of the body-focused movements did not reach a satisfactory reliability level.

Looking at movements from a different standpoint, the total time in movement increased in patients from a period of severe depression to one of almost complete recovery. From the first to the second of these periods the movements were also more complex, including more body areas (Fisch et al., 1983). Movements detected by the wrist sensor in the Kupfer et al. (1974) study showed unipolar depressives to be higher in activity level than bipolar depressives. The situation after three weeks of pharmacotherapy was very complicated. Overall, there were no significant differences, although there was a general rise in activity level. The complications become evident when we look at those who improve, compared with those who do not. Among the bipolar patients, the one (out of four) who did not improve had a slight decrease in activity; the others increased markedly, but were not analyzed separately. The unipolars either improved or worsened: The former showed a significant *decrease* in activity level, whereas the latter *increased*. The significance levels of these complex interactions were not assessed, as no overall analysis of the results was conducted.

In eye contact, the finding of less looking when depressed is replicated in five studies (Bouhuys & Alberts, 1984; Hinchliffe et al., 1971; Rutter & Stephenson, 1972; Rutter, 1976; Waxer, 1974b). Rutter & Stephenson compared depressive and schizophrenic patients with normal controls, and found the patient groups to be very similar on the looking dimension, except that the schizophrenics looked in rather shorter glances than did the depressives. In the later study, Rutter again found depressive and schizophrenic patients similar in looking, but only when talking with a normal, nonpatient conversational partner. When talking with another patient, the depressed patients looked less than the schizophrenic patients.

These, then, are the substantive findings on body movement in affective disorders. They are fairly consistent, and do not deviate much from the commonsense expectations, stated at the beginning of this section. Practically all the studies have focused on depressive patients' movements; we have so few results on manic patients that generalizations about them are not warranted. And only a couple of the publications go into the further classifications of unipolar and bipolar depression, so we cannot draw any conclusions about their movement patterns either.

OUTLINE OF AN APPLIED RESEARCH PROGRAM

While the research findings do seem to add up to the possibility of using nonverbal behaviors as cues to diagnosing affective disorders, the evidence is far from extensive, and there many missing components. The research program to be outlined here should be able to fill these gaps, and determine what steps must be taken to develop a system of nonverbal patient data acquisition to be used as an adjunct to other diagnostic procedures. It should be an extension of the diagnostic criteria in DSM-III, not a substitute for them. Again, this effort will be as practical as possible, and the final result should fit the diagnostic situation without too much extra burden—otherwise, no one will find it worthwhile to try fitting it in at all.

This outline will concentrate on the types of data that need to be collected to make the picture complete. Research designs will not be discussed; they need to meet the usual criteria of scientific excellence. The outline will address (1) patient sampling, (2) body movement sampling, and (3) methods of detecting and recording movements.

1. From what we have learned from the published studies of body movement in affective disorders, the obvious area of concentration in patient sampling will

be in representing the whole spectrum of affective disorders, not merely depression. Manic patients must be included, and among the depressive, some effort at sampling unipolar and bipolar depressions must be made. It may not be possible to have equal numbers of patients from these subcategories in each study, nor may it be wise: The main point is representativeness, based on the best epidemiological data available. Other variables for sampling will be the usual ones—sex, age, socioeconomic status, and so on.

2. Which body movements to focus on is less clear. The studies I have reviewed have covered only a few possibilities, perhaps important ones; and yet they seem to have been selected the basis of commonsense notions of depression more than on any theory of how depressed people should be expected to behave—and again, depressed people are virtually the only ones in the spectrum of affective disorders who have been studied at all. In short, a good deal more work needs to be done to identify those movements and postures that really differentiate patients with affective disorders from other patients. It may be that the movements and postures that have been studied will prove to be the correct ones, but the body of this literature is too thin for us to be sure at this time.

How does one mount a series of research studies to learn what the important movement and posture categories are? We are not completely in the dark about where to start; there are some theories about affective disorders to guide us, and there are some data-based expectations of the sorts of movements and other motor behaviors that might follow. The choice of theories is perhaps richer in the case of affective disorders than for other functional disorders. Biochemical, social, learning, psychoanalytic, and other theories have vied with each other in different contexts. All could be called upon for deductions about motor behaviors that should be expected. Many of these deductions may still sound like commonsense conclusions, but some surprises might also be found. The twin guiding principles should be consistency with the theory and practicality of measurement in clinical situations. In addition, investigators are beyond the piece-meal approach of trying out one motor behavior with a few patients, then another in the next little study, so that comparisons are hard to make. The studies should be sizeable and well-conducted so that some real conclusions can be drawn.

3. The methods for detecting the motor behaviors of interest should be as simple as possible. If we are to attend to these behaviors at all, both experimentation and practice will become more complicated. The extra pair of eyes owned by someone who is not simultaneously doing the interviewing, for example, is itself an enormous complication—it appears to raise the required personnel by a factor of two! On the other hand, incorporating motion-analysis equipment that feeds into sophisticated computer graphics can only serve a research purpose, and in some cases be an aid to training. Those results, in turn, will need to be interpreted. Some other technical equipment, such as stabilimeters, for example, could provide read-outs that can be easily interpolated into other data.

Even with this emphasis on simplicity, attention to body movements as a diagnostic adjunct is bound to complicate the procedure. If we follow the reasoning and evidence presented in the previous section, Personnel to Identify Movement, exhortations to the interviewer to attend to bodily expression will not be useful. An independent observer is a necessity, whether or not he or she has videotape recordings to go by. Motion sensors do not require that extra person, but we do not know yet whether the output from that technology will add substantially to the diagnostic process.

With this warning in mind, we should note that both the amount and the quality of information an observer can obtain are both very high. With judicious time sampling, the observer need be on duty at carefully selected times, and those shorter times can still yield good data.

It may be tempting to make the results of this research program into a prescription for diagnosis in the affective disorders. It would be difficult, however, for the whole mental-health field to adopt any set method of analysis or reporting. Indeed, many workers would resist it, often for very good reasons. A *method* should be the goal, one that can be applied within many clinical settings and yet be comparable across settings, even though specifics may differ.

ACKNOWLEDGMENT

My thanks to Louise Marshall, who provided access to a computer search of the relevant literature.

REFERENCES

American Psychiatric Association (1980). *Diagnostic and statistical manual on mental disease (third edition).* Washington, DC: American Psychiatric Association.

Bell, R. Q. (1968). Adaptation of small wrist watches for mechanical recording of activity in infants and children. *Journal of Experimental Child Psychology, 6,* 302–305.

Bouhuys, A. L. (1984). Observable behaviour as a predictor of improvement in endogenous depressive patients. In M. Hautzinger & R. Straub (Eds.) *Psychologische Asptekte depressiver Storungen* (pp. 27–51). Regensburg: Roderer.

Bouhuys, A. L., & Alberts, E. (1984). An analysis of the organization of looking and speech-pause behaviour of depressive patients. *Behaviour, 89,* 269–298.

Broadbent, D. E. (1958). *Perception and communication.* Oxford: Pergamon Press.

Broadbent, D. E. (1971). *Decision and stress.* London: Academic Press.

Dittmann, A. T. (1972). *Interpersonal messages of emotion.* New York: Springer Publishing Co.

Dittmann, A. T. (1977). The development of conversational behavior. In N. Freedman & S. Grand (Eds.), *Communicative structures and psychic structures: A psychoanalytic interpretation of communication* (pp. 133–147). New York: Plenum.

Dittmann, A. T. (1978). The role of body movement in communication. In A. W. Siegman & S. Feldstein (Eds.), *Nonverbal behavior and communication* (pp. 69–95). Hillsdale, NJ: Lawrence Erlbaum Associates.

Dittmann, A. T., & Goodrich, D. W. (1961). A comparison of social behavior in normal and hyperaggressive boys. *Child Development, 32*, 315–327.

Dittmann, A. T., & Llewellyn, L. G. (1969). Body movement and speech rhythm in social conversation. *Journal of Personality and Social Psychology, 11*, 98–106.

Dittmann, A. T., Parloff, M. B., & Boomer, D. S. (1965). Facial and bodily expression: A study of receptivity of emotional cues. *Psychiatry, 28*, 239–244.

Ekman, P., & Friesen, W. V. (1969). The repertoire of nonverbal behavior: Categories, usage, and coding. *Semiotica, 1*, 49–98.

Ekman, P., & Friesen, W. V. (1974). Nonverbal behavior and psychopathology. In R. J. Friedman & M. N. Mintz (Eds.), *The psychology of depression* (pp. 203–224). Washington, D. C.: V. H. Winston.

Fairbanks, L. A., McGuire, M. T., Cole, S. R., Sbordone, R., Silves, F. M., Richards, M., & Akers, J. (1977). The ethological study of four psychiatric wards: Patient, staff, and systematic behaviors. *Journal of Psychiatric Research, 13*, 193–209.

Fairbanks, L. A., McGuire, M. T., & Harris, C. J. (1982). Nonverbal interaction of patients and therapists during psychiatric interviews. *Journal of Abnormal Psychology, 91*, 109–119.

Fisch, H.-U., Frey, S., & Hirsbrunner, H.-P. (1983). Analyzing nonverbal behavior in depression. *Journal of Abnormal Psychology, 92*, 308–318.

Foshee, J. G. (1958). Studies in activity level. I. Simple and complex task performance in defectives. *American Journal of Mental Deficiency, 62*, 882–896.

Foster, F. G., Kupfer, D., Weiss, G., Lipponen, V., McPartland, R., & Delgado, J. (1972). Mobility recording and cycle research in neuropsychiatry. *Journal of Interdisciplinary Cycle Research, 3*, 61–72.

Freedman, N. (1972). The analysis of movement behavior during the clinical interview. In A. W. Siegman & B. Pope (Eds.), *Studies in dyadic communication* (pp. 153–175). New York: Pergamon Press.

Freedman, N., & Hoffman, S. P. (1967). Kinetic behavior in altered clinical states: Approach to objective analysis of motor behavior during clinical interviews. *Perceptual and Motor Skills, 24*, 527–539.

Greden, J. F., & Carroll, B. J. (1981). Psychomotor function in affective disorders: An overview of new monitoring techniques. *American Journal of Psychiatry, 183*, 1441–1448.

Guttman, H. A., Spector, R. M., Sigal, J. J., Rakoff, V., & Epstein, W. B. (1971). Reliability of coding affective communications in family therapy sessions: Problems of measurement and interpretation. *Journal of Consulting and Clinical Psychology, 37*, 397–402.

Hagan, R. L., Craighead, W. E., & Paul, G. L. (1975). Staff reactivity to evaluative behavioral observations. *Behavior Therapy, 6*, 201–205.

Haggard, E. A., & Isaacs, K. S. (1966). Micromomentary facial expressions as indicators of ego mechanisms in psychotherapy. In L. A. Gottschalk & A. H. Auerbach (Eds.), *Methods of research in psychotherapy* (pp. 154–165). New York: Appleton-Century-Crofts.

Hinchliffe, M. K., Lancashire, M., & Roberts, F. J. (1971). A study of eye-contact changes in depressed and recovered psychiatric patients. *British Journal of Psychiatry, 119*, 213–215.

Hinchliffe, M., Hooper, D., Roberts, F. J., & Vaughn, P. W. (1975) A study of the interaction between depressed patients and their spouses. *British Journal of Psychiatry, 126*, 164–172.

Johnson, H. G., Ekman, P., & Friesen, W. V. (1975). Communicative body movements: American emblems. *Semiotica, 15*, 335–353.

Johnson, S. M., & Bolstad, O. D. (1975). Reactivity to home observation: A comparison of audio recorded behavior with observers present or absent. *Journal of Applied Behavior Analysis, 8*, 181–185.

Jones, J. H., & Pansa, M. (1979). Some nonverbal aspects of depression and schizophrenia occurring during the interview. *Journal of Nervous and Mental Disease, 167*, 402–409.

Kent, R. N., & Foster, S. L. (1977). Direct observational procedures: Methological issues in naturalistic settings. In A. R. Ciminero, K. S. Calhoun, & H. E. Adams (Eds.), *Handbook of behavioral assessment*. New York: Wiley.

Kent, R. N., O'Leary, K. D., Diament, C., & Dietz, A. (1974). Expectation biases in observational evaluation of therapy change. *Journal of Consulting and Clinical Psychology, 42*, 774–780.

Kiritz, S. A. (1971). Hand movement and clinical ratings at admission and discharge for hospitalized psychiatric patients. Unpublished doctoral dissertation, University of California, San Francisco. [*Dissertation Abstracts International*, 1973, *33* (Section B), 4511.]

Kupfer, D. J., Detre, T. P., Foster, F. G., Tucker, G. J., & Delgado, J. (1972). The application of Delgado's telemetric motility recorder to human studies. *Behavioral Biology, 7*, 585–590.

Kupfer, D. J., Weiss, B. L., Foster, F. G., Detre, T. P., Delgado, J., & McPartland, R. (1974). Psychomotor activity in affective states. *Archives of General Psychiatry, 30*, 765–768.

Lewis, M., & Wilson, L. (1970). Infant stabilimeter. *Journal of Experimental Child Psychology, 10*, 52–56.

McGuire, M. T., Fairbanks, L. A., Cole, S. R., Sbordone, R., Silves, F. M., Richards, M., & Akers, J. (1977). The ethological study of four psychiatric wards: Behavioral changes and assessment with new staff and new patients. *Journal of Psychiatric Research, 13*, 211–224.

Mercatoris, M. & Craighead, W. E. (1974). The effects of non-participant observation on teacher and pupil classroom behavior. *Journal of Educational Psychology, 66*, 512–519.

Moos, R. H. (1968). Behavioral effects of being observed: Reaction to a wireless radio transmitter. *Journal of Consulting and Clinical Psychology, 32*, 382–388.

Olson, W. (1929). *The measurement of nervous habits in normal children*. Minneapolis, MN: University of Minnesota Press.

Purcell, K., & Brady, K. (1966). Adaptation to the invasion of privacy: Monitoring behavior with a miniature radio transmitter. *Merrill-Palmer Quarterly of Behavior and Development, 12*, 242–254.

Ranelli, C. J., & Miller, R. E. (1981). Behavior predictors of amitryptyline response in depression. *American Journal of Psychiatry, 138*, 30–34.

Rauch, M. D. (1953). An investigation of relationships between social behavior and psychiatric illness in hospitalized mental patients. Unpublished doctoral dissertation, University of California (Berkeley).

Rauch, S. S. (1953). The self-concept in relation to interpersonal attitudes and behavior in psychotic persons. Unpublished doctoral dissertation, University of California (Berkeley).

Raush, H. L. (1959). On the locus of behavior-observations in multiple settings within research treatment. *American Journal of Orthopsychiatry, 29*, 235–242.

Raush, H. L., Dittmann, A. T., & Taylor, T. J. (1959). Person, setting, and change in social interaction. *Human Relations, 12*, 361–378.

Reid, J. B. (1970). Reliability assessment of observation data: A possible methodological problem. *Child Development, 41*, 1143–1150.

Romanczyk, R. G., Kent, R. N., Diament, C., & O'Leary, K. D. (1973). Measuring the reliability of observational data: A reactive process. *Journal of Applied Behavior Analysis, 6*, 175–184.

Rosenfeld, H. M. (1982). Measurement of body motion and orientation. In K. R. Scherer and P. Ekman (Eds.), *Handbook of methods in nonverbal behavior research* (pp. 199–286). Cambridge: Cambridge University Press.

Rutter, D. R. (1976). Visual interaction in recently admitted and chronic longstay schizophrenic patients. *British Journal of Social and Clinical Psychology, 15*, 295–303.

Rutter, D. R., & Stephenson, G. M. (1972). Visual interaction in a group of schizophrenic and depressive patients. *British Journal of Social and Clinical Psychology, 11*, 57–65.

Sainsbury, P. (1955). Gestural movement during psychiatric interview. *Psychosomatic Medicine, 17*, 458–469.

Schulman, J. L., & Reisman, J. M. (1959). An objective measure of hyperactivity. *American Journal of Mental Deficiency, 64*, 455–456.

Steingart, I., & Freedman, N. (1975). The organization of body-focused kinesic behavior and language construction in schizophrenic and depressed states. *Psychoanalysis and Contemporary Science, 4*, 423–450.

Ulrich, G., & Harms, K. (1979). Video-analytic study of manual kinesics and its lateralization in the course of treatment of depressive syndromes. *Acta Psychiatrica Scandanavica, 59*, 481–492.

Waxer, P. H. (1974a). Therapist training in nonverbal communication: I. Nonverbal cues for depression. *Journal of Clinical Psychology, 30*, 215–218.

Waxer, P. (1974b). Nonverbal cues for depression. *Journal of Abnormal Psychology, 83*, 319–322.

Waxer, P. (1976). Nonverbal cues for depth of depression: Set versus no set. *Journal of Consulting and Clinical Psychology, 44*, 493.

Weik, K. E. (1968). Systematic observational methods. In G. Lindsey & E. Aronson (Eds.), *The handbook of social psychology* (Vol. II, pp. 357–451). Reading, MA: Addison-Wesley.

Youngren, M. A., & Lewinsohn, P. M. (1980). The functional relation between depression and problematic interpersonal behavior. *Journal of Abnormal Psychology, 89*, 333–341.

3 ASSESSMENT OF FACIAL BEHAVIOR IN AFFECTIVE DISORDERS

Paul Ekman
University of California, San Francisco

Alan J. Fridlund
The University of Pennsylvania

INTRODUCTION

This chapter suggests guidelines for measuring facial behavior in major affective disorders. We first discuss the relevance of facial expressions for studying major affective disorders. The two major decisions involved in examining facial behavior are described—selecting the conditions under which to obtain behavioral samples, and the methods for measuring the behavior. We then suggest priorities for research relating facial expressions to affective disorders, and we emphasize questions that must be addressed before clinical measurement of facial behavior is practical.

Clinical research on facial behavior in patients with different types of affective disorders is needed. This chapter provides clinical investigators with concepts and methods requisite for making informed decisions about measuring facial behavior. The chapter closes with a speculation of how the clinician of the future will use facial behavior in psychodiagnosis.

FACIAL EXPRESSIONS

It seems logical to measure the face in studies of affective disorders because the face is one of the main emotion signal systems. It is surprising that there have been so few studies on the topic (for reviews, see Ekman & Friesen, 1974; Fridlund, Ekman, & Oster, 1986; Jones, submitted for publication). The lack of adequate tools for measuring facial behavior is probably paramount in explaining the dearth of research. Research has also been limited by a failure to consider just how affective disorders might alter facial behavior.

Two issues need to be addressed to clarify the matter: First, we emphasize that facial behavior signals more than just emotion. Second, we distinguish among emotions, moods, emotional traits, and emotional disorders, considering how each of these phenomena may be manifested in facial behavior.

Types of Facial Actions

Some facial actions can signal emotion; most do not. Three types of facial actions are particularly relevant to affective disorders but do not signal emotion:

1. Instrumental facial actions such as lip-wiping and wetting often occur as anticholinergic side effects of antidepressant medication. Such actions should be monitored, but they should be separated from emotion signals.
2. "Emblematic" facial actions (Ekman, 1973) are socially learned, symbolic facial gestures whose meanings are widely shared within a culture. Examples include the wink, the facial shrug, and the tongue defiance display. These are premeditated, voluntary language-like facial expressions. We suggest that the frequency of emblematic actions drops with the onset of depression or increases in mania, and normalizes with clinical improvement. However, their occurrence in native-born Americans is infrequent and unlikely to contaminate facial behavior samples significantly. Studying emblematic actions in affective disorders may be more profitable in cultures where these behaviors are more frequent (e.g., Southern Italy).
3. Conversational facial signals (Ekman, 1979) include both the facial actions that punctuate spoken language and those made while listening. Conversational signals encourage a speaker to continue, call for more information, or presage an interruption. Ekman and Friesen (report to NIMH, 1982) found in a study of depressed and schizophrenic patients that conversational signals outnumbered emotion signals by a ratio of 3 to 1. The predominance of conversational signals prompted Fridlund and Gilbert (1985) to propose that the face be considered a "paralinguistic" display system.

Conversational signals, as important indices of social engagement, might be especially useful in diagnosing affective disorders, measuring their severity, and charting their course. We believe that depression is characterized by social disengagement and mania by hyperengagement. However, no research exists on conversational signals and affective disorders. Some of the facial measurement techniques described below can separate conversational from emotion signals. Other systems ignore the distinction and combine the two types of signals.

We focus primarily on techniques for measuring emotion using facial behavior because: (a) techniques for facial measurement were developed for studying emotion; (b) there is ample evidence that these techniques can accurately measure emotion; and (c) preliminary data suggest that these techniques are useful in studying affective disorders.

Distinguishing Facial Signs of Affective Phenomena

Facial behavior can be visible or invisible, because weak levels of facial muscular activity that produce no apparent movement are measurable with electromyography (EMG). In unpacking facial behavior we further distinguish (and suggest) the terms *expression configuration* (the specific muscles deployed in an expression) from *expression dynamics* (the amplitude-time course of the configuration; see Fridlund, Schwartz, & Fowler, 1984). Both properties are related to emotion: expression configuration specifies the type of emotion, and expression dynamics specify its strength.

There is consistent, robust evidence (see Fridlund, Ekman, & Oster, 1986, for the most recent review) for the facial configurations that signify fear, anger, disgust, contempt, combined sadness/distress, surprise, and happiness. Evidence is weaker for distinguishing guilt or shame from sadness/distress, and for measuring interest or different varieties of happiness (such as amusement, physical pleasure, and contentment).

There is less evidence about the dynamics of facial expressions. Two studies have shown that intensity and duration of muscular actions vary with strength of self-reported emotion (Ekman, Friesen, & Ancoli, 1980; Fridlund et al., 1984). Both configurative and dynamic features distinguish voluntarily-produced facial signals of emotion from more genuine, involuntary expressions (Ekman, Hager & Friesen, 1981; Ekman & Friesen, 1982; Ekman, 1984; Hager & Ekman, 1985). Voluntary-involuntary differences could be relevant for measuring emotions that a patient denies or is reluctant to disclose. These differences are strongest for happiness (Ekman & Friesen, 1982) but they may extend to other emotions as well.

In a study of archival records of depressed patients diagnosed according to DSM-II, Ekman, Matsumoto, and Friesen (1986) found that the distinction between voluntary and involuntary smiles was strongly related to diagnosis and improvement. Involuntary "felt" smiles were defined as expressions that involved both *zygomatic major* (the muscle that retracts the lip corners to form a smile) and *orbicularis oculi* (the eyelid muscle that lends the "crinkly-eye" appearance), whereas voluntary "unfelt" smiles involved only the *zygomatic major* without co-contractions of *orbicularis oculi*. Neurotic depressives showed more unfelt smiles than psychotic depressives on hospital admission, but the two groups were equivalent at discharge. Neurotic depressives showed more felt smiles than psychotic depressives at discharge, although the groups were equivalent on admission.

Other than those facial actions already prototypical of emotion, there is no evidence for any facial behaviors characteristic of moods, emotional traits or affective disorders. Ekman (1984) argued that these phenomena are likely to be characterized by unique facial dynamics but not configurations. Ekman distinguishes between an emotion (e.g., sadness/distress), a mood (feeling blue), an emotional trait (e.g., dysthymia) and an emotional disorder (depression).

"Blue" moods and clinical depressions are probably signalled by the occasions that produce certain facial configurations and the dynamics of these configurations (Ekman, 1984). In a blue mood, one readily feels sadness, and that emotion can be called forth easily. Periods of sadness will generally be longer and more intense than usual, and the sadness is more difficult to regulate, attenuate, or inhibit. These characteristics are even more pronounced in major affective disorders, in which affect can be "flooded" (Ekman & Friesen, 1975). Flooded affect emotions occur in response to events that are rarely evocative. They recur without apparent provocation, and their intensity and duration interfere with eating, working and sleeping.

DSM-III MAJOR AFFECTIVE DISORDERS AND EMOTION

In describing major affective disorders, DSM-III (American Psychiatric Association, 1980) specifies emotions, broad emotional features, and moods. Table 3.1 lists these affect-related terms; the relevant emotions are supplied paren-

TABLE 3.1
Affective Phenomena and DSM-III Criteria for Major Affective Disorders

	Major Depression	*Manic Episode*
Specific Emotions	Absence of pleasure (no happiness) Guilt	
Moods	Dysphoric (sadness/distress) Irritable (angry) Anxiety (fear)	Elevated (happiness) Irritable (angry) Dysphoric when not elevated or irritable
General Emotional Level	Agitated Retarded Anergic	

thetically. We note particularly that no specific affects are required for DSM-III diagnosis of major affective disorder. This nonspecificity in affect may reflect essential variability of emotion in major affective disorders, and with other evidence it forced Fridlund and Volpicelli (in preparation) to consider whether affective features are in fact a core property of depression and mania. The nonspecificity may also reflect subtypes of affective disorders, or previous unreliability in assessing emotions related to major affective disorders.

Specific emotions listed in Table 3.1 can be measured by most of the techniques described below. It is premature to focus exclusively on just those emotions. Research on facial behavior in affective disorders should include measurement of facial signals for all emotions, including disgust, contempt, and surprise. Table 3.1 also suggests the need to measure the range and dynamics of various facial configurations to achieve a measure of general emotionality. As mentioned previously, conversational signals are also useful as a measure of social disengagement or hyperengagement.

ALTERNATIVES FOR ELICITING FACIAL BEHAVIOR

Several clinical interaction formats allow sampling of facial behavior. Each has its own advantages and disadvantages. We consider four types, two of which are commonly part of clinical research: (1) unstructured clinical interviews; and (2) structured clinical interviews. The nonstandard procedures are: (3) structured imagery and reminiscence tasks, and (4) unobtrusive measurement of on-ward or on-site behavior. Unobtrusive measurement of facial behavior *in situ* is tactically impractical in most settings.

The first three methods require interaction of the patient with the clinician, and interaction with the professional may have a reactive impact upon the patient's facial behavior. Patients may show facial signs of "evaluation apprehension" (e.g., knitting of brows) or undue politeness (e.g., appeasement smiles), and depending on the patient, exaggeration or minimization of distress. It is unknown how a patient's tendency to exaggerate or minimize complaints affects facial behavior and psychodiagnosis. Nor is it known whether individuals with affective disorders show atypical responses in this interaction. In either case, patients' facial behavior while interacting with clinicians cannot be assumed to reflect a core property of affective disorder without unobtrusively verifying the behavior in nonclinical settings.

Any of the three interaction formats requires the investigator to choose whether to use a hidden or a visible camera. The hidden camera allows less reactive measurement of facial behavior, but it may pose problems in obtaining informed consent. The visible camera obviates difficulties in obtaining consent but may result in attenuated or distorted facial behavior (e.g., Kleck, Vaughan, Cartwright-Smith, Vaughan, Colby, & Lanzetta, 1976; however, note that such studies have not used patient populations), and its presence may harm some patients' treatment. Videotape or film recording may be employed; Walbott (1982) presents the advantages and constraints of each format.

Brief reviews of the three interaction formats for obtaining clinical samples of facial behavior follow.

Unstructured Clinical Interview

This most common psychodiagnostic method carries the advantages of varying length, the flexibility to explore in depth specific features of the patient's presentation, and the ability to elicit affect from a patient who would be unexpressive under more restrictive conditions. The unstructured interview has the severe drawbacks that facial behavior is likely to be very sparse, and, given the uniqueness of each interview, comparisons across individuals are nearly impossible.

Structured Clinical Interview

The structured interview (e.g., the SADS protocol) has the advantages that the interview format is relatively consistent, and patients' facial behaviors from question to question are more readily comparable. One liability of the structured interview is the inflexible transition that must occur between questions. From our viewing videotapes of SADS interviews with patients, we believe that these transitions can be jarring and often inhibit emotional expression. Like the unstructured interview, the structured interview readily yields conversational samples but still requires long recording epochs to obtain facial emotional behavior. Additionally, the optimal methods for parsing interview segments into behavioral samples are not known.

Imagery, Self-reference, and Reminiscence Tasks

Laboratory experiments on induced mood often use a variety of imagery, self-reference, or reminiscence tasks. In imagery tasks, patients may be asked to recall, then "re-experience", personally significant emotional events. Alternatively, they are asked to imagine "affective imagery" items culled from standardized protocols of everyday emotional situations. Self-reference tasks such as Velten statements rely on suggestion to elicit emotion ("I feel blue"). Imagery and self-reference tasks typically employ items or statements with known (or predictable) emotion content. Reminiscence tasks do not involve prior procurement of an "item" or "situation" for eliciting emotion; they rely on free recall by patients of material that may have varying, unpredictable emotion content.

Although imagery, self-reference, and reminiscence tasks seem to provide an easy way to elicit authentic emotion, closer analysis suggests otherwise. These tasks have in common the request by the experimenter or clinician to experience emotion. Thus any expressions of emotion induced in these procedures may be as reflective of compliance as of felt emotion, and inhibited or histrionically intensified facial behavior may occur. However, these tasks have an advantage over the structured clinical interview in that emotion elicitors may be more potent and the emotion content specified more precisely.

These structured tasks are all economical. They can be used to evoke emotion quickly and in a relatively controlled fashion, despite their confounding with effects of compliance. The twin advantages of economy and standardization are important when facial behavior is the major interest. Facial behavior is very densely packed. Whatever task is employed, acquiring and measuring the facial behavior will take considerable time. Therefore, brief sampling epochs are desirable, and the fact that standard tasks can fit into brief epochs is highly advantageous.

A disadvantage of imagery and self-referent tasks is that they exclude conversation, and facial conversational signs may change significantly in major affective disorders. Reminiscence tasks include conversation but typically do not use standardized emotion elicitors. A good compromise is to use imagery which is guided and constructed by the patient from personal experience. Facial behavior can be sampled during the imagery. The patient is then asked to recount his or her experience of the imagery, and conversational signals (possibly admixed with emotion signals) can be observed.

MEASUREMENT OF FACIAL ACTION

Many systems have been developed to structure and analyze observations of facial action. Ekman (1982) has provided a detailed comparison of fourteen major facial coding systems. Most evolved for studying emotion to the exclusion of nonemotional facial behavior. No facial measurement methods have been developed for studying psychopathology. As a result, theory and data are sparse concerning the relationship of emotional and nonemotional facial behaviors to major affective disorders.

Facial behavior, as previously mentioned, is densely packed. The face contains nearly 80 expressive muscles that act in rapidly changing patterns and which, by their co-contractions, can form tens of thousands of facial expressions. Consequently, choices about how much facial behavior to measure are crucial. Also crucial are choices about *which* facial behaviors to measure.

Table 3.2 diagrams the decisions facing the clinical investigator in choosing a facial measurement system. The first choice is whether facial behavior is to be measured comprehensively or selectively. In selective measurement, certain facial behaviors, or patterns of behaviors, are measured and the rest are excluded. Selective facial measurement is the method of choice whenever the behaviors to

TABLE 3.2
Decision Tree for Measuring Facial Behavior

- Breadth of Measurement
  - Comprehensive Facial Measurement
    - Direct Measurement (FACS)
    - Observer Open-Ended Inference
  - Selective Facial Measurement
    - Direct Measurement
      - Facial Coding (EMFACS, MAX, AFFEX)
      - Facial EMG
    - Observer Structured Inference (Emotion checklists, rating scales, inventories)

be measured can be specified in advance. However, it is not known what kinds of facial behavior are most likely to aid in diagnosing or quantifying the course of an affective disorder. This point underscores our earlier emphasis on measuring more than just emotions specified or implied by DSM-III. Comprehensive measurement is costly but in the present state of knowledge about facial behavior and affective disorders it is mandated. Furthermore, it is the only way to discover unexpected facial behavior correlates of affective disorders. Comprehensive measurement can be performed either using observers or by direct measurement of facial activity.

Comprehensive Facial Measurement

There are two major comprehensive methods of facial measurement. One uses open-ended inferences drawn by observers of facial behavior. The other measures facial behavior directly. Observers may be able to infer phenomena that no direct measurement system is yet configured to detect. On the other hand, detailed information that can be directly measured in the face may be missed by observers.

Open-ended Observation

Open-ended observers' reports about facial behavior are rarely employed. Yet they are among the simplest measurement methods, and they offer an unusually wide net with which to assay facial behaviors relevant to affective disorders. Observers are simply shown videotaped facial behavior. They are then asked to report what they see. Their responses are audiotaped and collated. The responses can be unstructured, or observers can be prompted to provide their judgments about "disorders," "moods," "traits," and "emotions." Systematically collecting observers' open-ended impressions would provide valuable data on how individuals perceive patients' affect. It allows one to incorporate in theory and research all reasonable inferences about facial behavior and affective disorders.

What kinds of observers should be used? We suspect that naive observers, trained nonexpert observers, and expert clinicians would provide different and complementary reports that could guide future hypothesis construction and testing. Should observers view videotapes that provide the full sound track? Past research has involved omitted or filtered speech or provided just the video image. However, we see no reason in initial research to forsake the ecological validity of the full audiovisual presentation. Including the sound track also simplifies separating conversational from emotional facial behaviors, and presently elicited from referential emotion (i.e., produced by memory or reflection).

Comprehensive Direct Measurement of Facial Behavior

In contrast to open-ended observation, in which observers supply impressions of facial behavior, here the behavior itself is measured. Comprehensive general-purpose direct facial coding is provided uniquely by Ekman and Friesen's Facial Action Coding System (FACS; Ekman & Friesen, 1976, 1978). Based on empirical findings, FACS includes 44 visibly-discriminable component facial behaviors which, singly or in combination, account for all visible facial movement. Within FACS, the component behaviors are called Action Units, or AUs. AUs are scoreable according to 5-point intensity ratings. Because the timing of muscular actions seems critical for discriminating types of facial behavior, FACS provides coding of AU dynamics, that is, timing of AU onset, apex and offset. High interrater reliabilities have been obtained using FACS.

FACS takes considerable time to learn and use, and it requires repeated, slow-motion viewing of facial actions. FACS is thus currently unsuitable for real-time coding. By its nature, FACS includes more distinctions than may be needed for assessing any one patient population. Initially its use increases the expense and tedium of measurement. However, once meaningful behavioral units are derived empirically, elementary measurement units can be collapsed and subtle distinctions disregarded. Flexibility in retaining and discarding AUs will be critical in early research on facial behavior and affective disorders, because initial hypotheses will be largely speculative.

Selective Facial Measurement

Several methods are available for measuring facial behavior selectively. Selective measures are economical because they exclude many types of facial behavior or its fine-grained features (e.g., expression dynamics). Selective measures are preferable when the facial behaviors of value are known in advance.

A major liability of these methods is that they were not developed for studying affective disorders. Their selectivity is usually based on theoretical preconceptions that may be irrelevant for diagnosing or charting the course of major affective disorders. They do not usually parse emotional from conversational facial behaviors, and some behaviors characteristic of emotion are omitted. Therefore, the bases for selecting and quantifying facial behaviors may not be optimal for studying affective disorders. Selective methods of facial measurement include both observer judgments and direct measurement. Selective direct measurement can be performed using either visual coding or facial electromyography.

Selective Observer Judgment

In the judgment approach, observers are asked to make judgments about slides, films, or occasionally, live presentations of facial expressions. For example, videotapes of depressed patients are shown to judges who are asked to classify each patient as having Major Depression with or without Melancholia. Judgment approaches typically involve placing expressions either along emotion scales (e.g., Schlosberg, 1941, 1952, 1954) or in discrete emotion categories (e.g., Izard, 1971, 1972, 1977; and see review of scaling and categorical approaches by Ekman, Friesen, & Ellsworth, 1982). They can equally well be used to assign individuals psychodiagnoses. Unlike open-ended observation, observer judgment methods by nature constrain observers' responses. The constraints on observer responses make judgment methods inappropriate for exploratory studies of facial behavior in affective disorders. Rather, construction of rating scales, categories, checklists, etc., should follow pilot research using comprehensive measurement.

Selective Direct Measurement

In the selective direct measurement approach, facial behaviors are specified in advance and sampled at a predetermined level of precision. Specification of behavioral units proceeds from theory, research or clinical inference. Selective direct measurement is performed using visible facial coding systems or by electromyography. Selective visible facial coding systems require a videotaped record of the patient's facial behavior. Electromyography does not require videotaping, but requires placement of recording electrodes for monitoring the patient's physiological activity.

MAX and AFFEX. The major exemplars of selective direct measurement facial coding systems are the Maximally Descriptive Facial Movement Coding System (MAX; Izard. 1979), the System for Identifying Affect Expression by Holistic Judgment (AFFEX; Izard & Dougherty, 1980), and the Emotion Facial Action Coding System (EMFACS; Friesen & Ekman, 1983). MAX and AFFEX are based on early recognition studies that established the universal association of certain facial expressions with specific emotions. Neither MAX nor AFFEX provides an exhaustive listing of possible facial behaviors. MAX, for example, provides only those 27 descriptors believed by Izard to be necessary to form judgments about seven "primary" emotions. No data are provided to show that the excluded facial actions do not reflect emotion. Thus whether the systems exhaustively measure facial behavior relevant to major affective disorder cannot be internally confirmed or disconfirmed. Expression dynamics are disregarded; facial behavior is instead seen as "on" or "off."

EMFACS. EMFACS represents Ekman and Friesen's desire to supplement the comprehensive FACS with a standardized selective alternative that measures broader, emotion-related facial actions. EMFACS considers only emotional expressions, and among those only the AUs and AU combinations best supported by empirical findings or theory as emotion signals. Like MAX and AFFEX, EMFACS is a selective direct measurement coding system, but with an important difference—its systematic derivation from FACS permits confident statements about its omissions. The solidity of EMFACS' empirical grounding is suggested by numerous concurrent validation studies with FACS. These indicate high correlations (>.8) of EMFACS and FACS codings.

Coding time with EMFACS is speeded, albeit at the expense of subtler AUs and AU combinations, including those indicative of conversational signals or selfmanipulations. Precise temporal dynamics of the facial actions are replaced by unitary demarcations of peak actions. To maintain an empirical approach in EMFACS scoring, facial actions are, like FACS, described in terms of numerical codes. Coders are also requested not to interpet actions as emotion signals until they are tabulated *post hoc* and classified according to EMFACS criteria.

Although not all FACS emotion hypotheses have been tested, a number of predictions have been supported (see review by Ekman, 1982). Studies of spontaneous emotional expression using self report as a validity criterion support predictions about actions that signal happiness, fear, distress, and disgust. Studies employing observers' attributions of emotion as a validity criterion support FACS predictions for these emotions as well as for surprise and anger.

Before considering the alternative technique for selective direct facial measurement—electromyography—we consider two pilot studies of facial behavior and affective disorders to illustrate the utility of FACS and EMFACS.

Ekman and Friesen (report to NIMH, 1981) used FACS to measure the facial behavior shown by patients on admission to an inpatient psychiatric facility. All facial movement during the first 8 questions and the last 5 questions in a standard interview was measured. The DSM-II diagnoses of the patients were: major depressive (N = 4), minor depressive (N = 3), manic (N = 3), and schizophrenic (N = 2). Results reflect combined scores from the two interview samples.

FACS measurements identified 5,987 separate expressions. Some were composed of one muscular action; others involved co-contractions of 2 to 5 muscles.

About one third (1770) of these expressions involved actions predicted by FACS to signal emotion. Most frequent were nonemotional facial actions such as lowering or raising the eyebrows to punctuate speech.

Figure 3.1 shows that patients diagnosed with major depression showed more sadness and disgust and fewer unfelt-happy expressions than minor depressives. Manics showed more felt-happy, unfelt-happy and fewer anger, disgust or sadness expressions than either depression group. Schizophrenics differed from manics and depressives in showing more fear expressions and fewer of the other emotional expressions. Figure 3.2 shows emotion scores for each of the four patients with major depression. Individual differences are apparent for sadness (fewer for patient 38) and unfelt happy (more for patient 10) expressions.

Patient groups also differed in their nonemotional speech-punctuating facial movements. Depressives and schizophrenics showed fewer speech-punctuating facial movements than manics. Major depressives showed much more brow lowering than brow raising in punctuating speech than the other groups, whereas manics showed the opposite pattern.

This study shows the feasibility and promise of facial measurement in diagnosing affective disorder, although small sample sizes prevented drawing firm conclusions. Nor was it possible to evaluate whether facial measurements at admission predicted clinical improvement.

Ekman, Matsumoto, & Friesen (1986) used EMFACS to score facial behavior of psychiatric inpatients filmed by Ekman and Friesen in 1964. Patients were

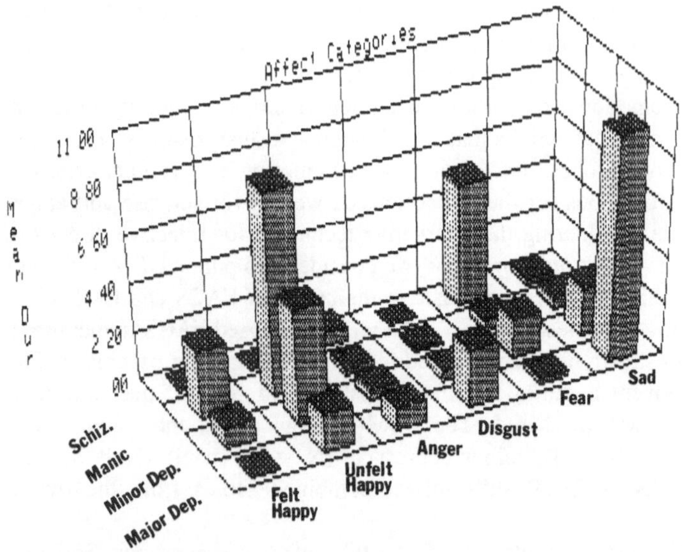

FIGURE 3.1. Mean duration of affect for psychiatric groups.

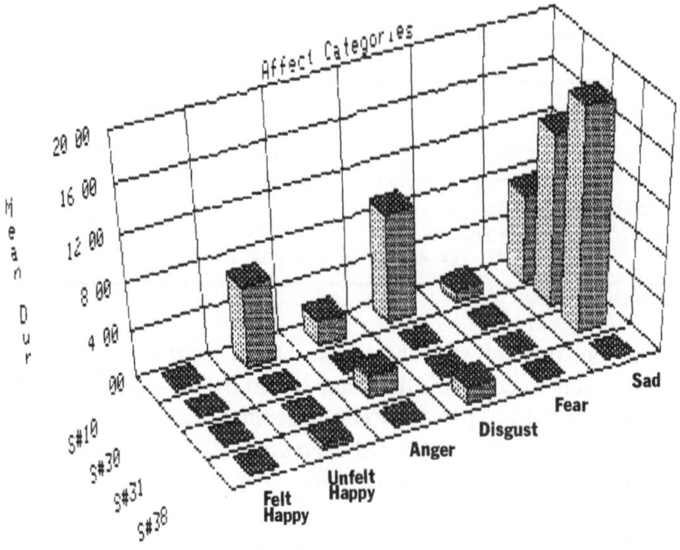

FIGURE 3.2. Mean duration of affect for major depressives.

filmed during standardized interviews at admission and at discharge. For 17 patients the attending physician and the ward chief agreed by the time of discharge on a DSM-II depression diagnosis. Mean age of these patients at time of admission to the hospital was 47.5 years. Patients' hospital stays averaged 68 days.

Brief Psychiatric Rating Scale (BPRS) ratings were made independently by three clinical psychologists after viewing the first 2 minutes of the admission interview. They then viewed the first 2 minutes of the discharge film. They made a second set of BPRS ratings, and also rated each patient on degree of clinical improvement. A single coder measured facial behavior with EMFACS. A second reliability coder independently measured the facial behavior shown by 8 of the patients in focal 1-minute interview samples. Intercoder reliability of EMFACS was .821.

Table 3.3 shows that more felt-happy expressions and fewer unfelt-happy expressions occurred at discharge relative to admission. The number of sad expressions tended to decrease, but the change was not significant. Patients who showed sadness expressions were rated by the clinicians as less disturbed (lower BPRS scores), both at admission and discharge (Table 3.4). At admission patients who showed sad expressions did so when describing current feelings. At discharge patients who showed sad expressions did so when describing how they *had* felt when admitted. Sadness at admission did not predict clinical improvement by discharge (Table 3.4).

TABLE 3.3
Number of Patients showing Happy Facial Expressions in Admission and Discharge Interviews

	Interviews	
	Admission	*Discharge*
Felt-happy expressions	3	12
Unfelt-happy expressions	14	5
$X^2 = 9.63$, df = 1, $p = .01$		

On admission, patients who showed at least one happy expression (felt- or unfelt-happy), were rated as less disturbed (mean BPRS = 30.5) than those who did not (mean BPRS 43.2, $p <.01$). This difference was independent of whether they also showed a negative emotional expression. There was almost no overlap (1 of 17 subjects) in BPRS score distributions of those who did and did not show a happy expression.

Contempt expressions and unfelt-happy expressions at admission were independently associated with *less* clinical improvement. Each expression correlated with improvement even when variance associated with the other emotion was statistically removed (Table 3.5). Severity of disturbance on the BPRS at admission was positively correlated with subsequent clinical improvement. Table 3.5 shows that when unfelt-happy and contempt expression scores at admission were added to the BPRS scores in a multiple correlation with clinical improvement, the correlation was significant. Expression scores explained 46% of the variance. When expression scores were entered first in the multiple correlation, they correlated .79 ($p < .001$) with subsequent clinical improvement. Adding the BPRS accounted for only 4% of predicted variance.

Findings from this study are very promising but are limited in two regards. First, patients were not diagnosed using DSM-III. Second, the expert BPRS

TABLE 3.4
BPRS Ratings of Patients who Did or Did Not Show Any Sadness Expressions

	BPRS Rating			
	Admission Interview		*Discharge Interview*	
	Mean	*SD*	*Mean*	*SD*
Sadness expressions	32.8	8.1	19.5	1.6
No sadness expressions	38.5	7.7	24.5	5.5
p (two-tailed)	.03		.01	

TABLE 3.5
Correlations Between Facial Emotion Scores on Admission and Ratings of Subsequent Clinical Improvement

	Rank Order Correlation	*Partial Correlation*
Contempt	$-.54\ p < .05$	$-.69\ p < .002$ (controlling for Unfelt-happy)
Unfelt-happy	$-.60\ p < .01$	$-.71\ p < .001$ (controlling for Contempt)

ratings of severity and clinical improvement were made after observing only two minutes of interview behavior. Despite these limitations, this pilot study shows the feasibility and clinical relevance of directly measuring facial behavior during standard interviews.

Facial Electromyography. Now we consider the alternative method for selective direct facial measurement, facial electromyography (EMG). Fridlund and Izard (1983) presented principles of facial EMG and reviewed the relevant literature. Fridlund and Cacioppo (in preparation) presented general guidelines for electromyographic research. In facial EMG, sensitive amplifiers detect tiny electrical discharges generated by contracting facial muscles. Contact with the muscle tissue can be made directly by using indwelling fine wires. More frequently, recording proceeds indirectly through skin, using surface electrodes filled with conductive paste and attached to the skin with adhesive collars.

Facial EMG has three advantages over direct observation of the face. First, the EMG signal is instantaneously detectable and thereby lends itself to immediate recording. Second, the EMG signal offers a more finely graded measure of muscle activity than can be provided by visible facial coding systems or observer judgments. Third, EMG techniques detect muscle contractions that are too small to be observable (see Ekman, 1982). This advantage may be important in assessing "covert" emotional signals or mood states.

There are several disadvantages to the use of facial EMG. Recording facial EMG requires an extensive electrode application procedure. For this reason,

TABLE 3.6
Severity and Emotion Measures at Admission and Clinical Improvement

Measure at Admission	
BPRS	$r = .46, p = .06$
BPRS + contempt + unfelt happy	$R = .82, p = .005$
Unfelt happy + contempt	$R = .79, p = .001$
Unfelt happy + contempt + BPRS	$R = .82, p = .001$

recording from more than three or four facial sites at one sitting is likely to be too time-consuming and stressful for the patient. Because the electrodes make direct contact with the face, the patient is usually manifestly aware that he/she is participating in research concerning the face. The patient's self-consciousness can result in distorted or attenuated facial behavior (Fridlund & Izard, 1983; Kleck et al., 1976). The leads, paste, and collars inhibit movement and may be torn by strong muscle actions. Attaching the recording discs can be problematic on males with heavy beard growth. If fine-wire recording is performed, implantation of the electrodes often produces irritation and pain.

Nor can a facial EMG signal be taken necessarily as an accurate representation of ongoing dynamic muscle activity. The relationship between detected electrical output at an EMG site, and the mechanical force exerted by a muscle, may change over time as a function of fatigue (Mulder & Hulstijn, 1984).

Given the practical limits on number of electrodes that can be applied, careful *a priori* judgments must be made about which facial sites to monitor. Facial EMG is therefore a selective direct measurement method.

Facial EMG has the additional drawback that conversational and emotional signals cannot be distinguished without an accompanying audio record. The typical surface electrodes used in facial EMG recording show pickup areas considerably broader than the muscles directly underlying the electrode site, and thus facial actions signifying emotion may be confused with conversational signals from other muscles. Care should also be used in processing EMG signals to insure that expression dynamics are not obscured by over-averaging of the signals (see Fridlund, 1979).

Facial EMG measurement is most applicable when the investigator can specify in advance the emotions and/or facial actions of interest, when unobtrusiveness is not crucial, and when the subject is not called upon to move the face or body excessively. EMG is probably most useful in the structured imagery and reminiscence tasks described above. Facial EMG may also be the only method of ascertaining whether patients with major affective disorders show chronic facial behavior which is too weak to be visible.

To date, facial EMG techniques have been used to study affective imagery and mood states (Brown & Schwartz, 1980; Carney, Hong, O'Connell, & Amado, 1981; Fridlund, Schwartz, & Fowler, 1984; Oliveau & Willmuth, 1979; Schwartz, Brown, & Ahern, 1980; Schwartz, Fair, Mandel, Salt, & Klerman, 1976a,b; Schwartz, Fair, Mandel, Salt, Mieske, & Klerman, 1978; Teasdale & Bancroft, 1977; Teasdale & Rezin, 1978); posed expressions (Rusalova, Izard, & Simonov, 1975; Sumitsuji, Matsumoto, Tanaka, Kashiwagi, & Kaneko, 1967, 1977); and social interaction and empathy (Cacioppo & Petty, 1979; Englis, Vaughan, & Lanzetta, 1982; Vaughan & Lanzetta, 1980, 1981). Facial EMG research on "depression" (usually measured only by self-report inventory) suggests that EMG may usefully quantify dysphoria. Its relevance for DSM-III major affective disorder is unknown.

RECOMMENDATIONS FOR RESEARCH ON FACIAL BEHAVIOR AND AFFECTIVE DISORDERS

Analyzing facial behavior in major affective disorder patients can uncover new phenomena about affective disorders, and substantiate clinical inferences regarding their relationships with emotion. Such research may enable refinement of diagnosis and more accurate measurement of treatment effects and clinical improvement. Comprehensive measurement (both direct measurement and open-ended observation) is a priority for initial research. It is more costly at the outset, but it is the only way to discover exactly which facial behaviors are most relevant to affective disorders. It may be the most cost-effective in the long run. Selective measurement approaches have a rightful place in follow-up research.

Another priority is determining how various types of standardized tasks compare to structured interviews in eliciting facial behavior useful for diagnosing and charting the course of affective disorders.

Specific attention should be directed toward measuring what we term expression dynamics (especially facial action timing) to determine whether there are patterns that characterize affective disorders but not emotions, moods or traits. Basic psychophysical studies using facial behaviors and observer judgments are needed to ascertain what configurations and dynamics are necessary for ascription of the terms "mood," "trait," or "disorder." This type of research can discover naturalistically how clinicians already assess emotion in affective disorders, and it will enable better clinical training in discriminating affective phenomena in and apart from affective disorders.

There is considerable clinical speculation regarding the psychodynamics of depression. Analytic theorists have posited retroflected anger and lowered self-esteem in the etiology. Learned helplessness accounts suggest that incipient coping attempts are neutralized by anticipation of defeat and futility of action. These hypotheses may be tested by examining the fleeting "micromomentary" expressions (Ekman & Friesen, 1969) that indicate transient affects and which can only be detected using detailed facial coding procedures. For example, the retroflected anger account might predict that the depressed patient would show micromomentary anger, contempt or disgust signals immediately followed by signals of guilt, fear or shame. Regardless of whether these signals were micromomentary in nature, the sequencing of emotional expressions in major affective disorders might decode underlying psychodynamics.

We reiterate our concern that studies of facial behavior in affective disorders parse conversational from emotional signals. This will allow separate assessment of predominance of emotion in affective disorders from the social disengagement (or hyperengagement) seen in such patients.

Recommending that practitioners measure facial behavior is premature. The task is still too costly. Answers must first be obtained to questions we have raised about eliciting, selecting, and sampling facial behavior in the ways most useful for diagnosis and therapy. The measurement tools are ready, the questions are posed, and the answers can be found in the near future. A conjecture about what may then result follows.

A GLIMPSE OF THE NOT TOO DISTANT FUTURE

The last item on the standardized intake questionnaire tells Ms. R to turn on the TV set, and put on the headphones. A series of six one-minute films, each evoking a different emotion, appears on the screen. After each film Ms. R is instructed to rate how she felt while watching each film. After the last film rating, Ms. R hears a brief burst of white noise.

The videocamera mounted in the video monitor transmits her facial expressions to a video digitizer/frame grabber. A pattern recognition program sorts the resulting pixel representation of her facial movements into action units. SQUID (superconducting quantum interference device) sensors monitor her heart rate, brain waves, and respiration remotely. A thermal camera records changes in her facial blood flow and skin temperature. A mathematical pattern classifier (see Fridlund et al., 1984) integrates these data to yield the facial/autonomic pattern and strength of response to each emotional challenge, calibrated against Ms. R's general arousal measured during startle. This output, combined with an endocrine panel and polysomnogram, provides a profile of affective status. A computerized expert system suggests numerically probable diagnoses and treatment options.

REFERENCES

American Psychiatric Association. (1980). *Diagnostic and statistical manual of mental disorders.* Washington, DC: Author.

Brown, S. L., & Schwartz, G. E. (1980). Relationships between facial electromyography and subjective experience during affective imagery. *Biological Psychology, 11,* 49–62.

Cacioppo, J. T., & Petty, R. E. (1979). Attitudes and cognitive response: An electrophysiological approach. *Journal of Personality and Social Psychology, 37,* 2181–2199.

Carney, R. M., Hong, B. A., O'Connell, M. F., & Amado, H. (1981). Facial electromyography as a predictor of treatment outcome in depression. *British Journal of Psychiatry, 138,* 454–459.

Ekman, P. (1973). Cross cultural studies of facial expressions. In P. Ekman (Ed.), *Darwin and facial expression* (pp. 169–229). New York: Academic Press.

Ekman, P. (1979). About brows: Emotional and conversational signals. In M. von Cranach, K. Foppa, W. Lepenies, & D. Ploog (Eds.), *Human ethology* (pp. 169–248). Cambridge: Cambridge University Press.

Ekman, P. (1982). Methods for measuring facial action. In K. R. Scherer & P. Ekman (Eds.), *Handbook of methods in nonverbal behavior research* (pp. 45–90). New York: Cambridge University Press.

Ekman, P. (1984). Expression and the nature of emotion. In K. R. Scherer & P. Ekman (Eds.), *Approaches to emotion* (pp. 319–344). Hillsdale, N.J.: Lawrence Erlbaum Associates.

Ekman, P., & Friesen, W. V. (1969). Nonverbal leakage and clues to deception. *Psychiatry, 32*, 88–105.

Ekman, P., & Friesen, W. V. (1974). Nonverbal behavior and psychopathology. In R. J. Friedman & M. M. Katz (Eds.), *The psychology of depression: Contemporary theory and research* (pp. 203–232). Washington, D. C.: Winston & Sons.

Ekman, P., & Friesen, W. V. (1975). *Unmasking the face*. Englewood Cliffs, NJ: Prentice-Hall.

Ekman, P., & Friesen, W. V. (1976). Measuring facial movement. *Journal of Environmental Psychology and Nonverbal Behavior, 1*, 56–75.

Ekman, P., & Friesen, W. V. (1978). *The Facial Action Coding System*. Palo Alto, California: Consulting Psychologists Press.

Ekman, P., & Friesen, W. V. (1981). Final report to the National Institute of Mental Health, Collaborative studies on depression. (Contract No. HSM 42–72–213(ER).)

Ekman, P., & Friesen, W. V. (1982). Felt, false, and miserable smiles. *Journal of Nonverbal Behavior, 6*, 238–252.

Ekman, P., Matsumoto, D., & Friesen, W. V. (1986). Facial Expression in affective disorders. Unpublished manuscript.

Ekman, P., Friesen, W. V., & Ancoli, S. (1980). Facial signs of emotional experience. *Journal of Personality and Social Psychology, 39*, 1125–1134.

Ekman, P., Friesen, W. V., & Ellsworth, P. (1982). What emotion categories or dimensions can observers judge from facial behavior? In P. Ekman (Ed.), *Emotion in the human face* (2nd Ed.) (pp. 39–55). Cambridge: Cambridge University Press.

Ekman, P., Hager, J. C., & Friesen, W. V. (1981). The symmetry of emotional and deliberate facial actions. *Psychophysiology, 18*, 101–106.

Englis, B. G., Vaughan, K. B., & Lanzetta, J. T. (1982). Conditioning of counterempathetic emotional responses. *Journal of Experimental Social Psychology, 38*, 375–391.

Fridlund, A. J. (1979). Contour-following integrator for dynamic tracking of electromyographic data. *Psychophysiology, 16*, 491–493.

Fridlund, A. J., & Gilbert, A. N. (1985). Emotion and facial expression. *Science, 230*, 607–608.

Fridlund, A. J., & Cacioppo, J. T. (1986). Publication guidelines for research involving electromyography. Society for Psychophysiological Research.

Fridlund, A. J., Ekman, P., & Oster, H. (1987). Facial expressions of emotion: Review of literature, 1970–1983. In A. Siegman & S. Feldstein (Eds.), *Nonverbal behavior and communication* (2nd Ed.). Hillsdale, N. J.: Lawrence Erlbaum Associates.

Fridlund, A. J., & Izard, C. E. (1983). Electromyographic studies of facial expressions of emotions and patterns of emotions. In J. T. Cacioppo & R. E. Petty (Eds.), *Social psychophysiology: A sourcebook* (pp. 243–286). New York: Guilford Press.

Fridlund, A. J., Schwartz, G. E., & Fowler, S. C. (1984). Pattern recognition of self-reported emotional state from multiple-site facial EMG activity during affective imagery. *Psychophysiology, 21*, 622–637.

Fridlund, A. J., & Volpicelli, J. (in preparation). Depression is not an affective disorder.

Friesen, W. V., & Ekman, P. (1983). *EMFACS*. Mimeographed document. San Francisco: Human Interaction Laboratory.

Hager, J. C., & Ekman, P. (1985). The asymmetry of facial actions is inconsistent with models of hemispheric specializations. *Psychophysiology, 22*, 307–318.

Izard, C. E. (1971). *The face of emotion*. New York: Appleton-Century-Crofts.

Izard, C. E. (1972). *Patterns of emotion: A new analysis of anxiety and depression*. New York: Academic Press.

Izard, C. E. (1977). *Human emotions*. New York: Plenum.

Izard, C. E. (1979). *The maximally discriminative facial movement coding system (MAX)*. Newark, Delaware: Instructional Resources Center, University of Delaware.

Izard, C. E., & Dougherty, L. M. (1980). *System for identifying affect expressions by holistic judgment (AFFEX)*. Newark, Delaware: Instructional Resources Center, University of Delaware.

Jones, I. H. (Manuscript submitted for publication). Nonverbal behavior—A review of the literature in clinical populations.

Kleck, R. E.,Vaughan, R. C., Cartwright-Smith, J., Vaughan, K. B., Colby, C. Z., & Lanzetta, J. T. (1976). Effects of being observed on expressive, subjective, and physiological responses to painful stimuli. *Journal of Personality and Social Psychology, 34*, 1211–1218.

Mulder, T., & Hulstijn, W. (1984). The effects of fatigue and task repetition on the surface electromyographic signal. *Psychophysiology, 21*, 528–534.

Oliveau, D., & Willmuth, R. (1979). Facial muscle electromyography in depressed and non-depressed hospitalized subjects: A partial replication. *American Journal of Psychiatry, 136*, 548–550.

Rusalova, M. N., Izard, C. E., & Simonov, P. V. (1975). Comparative analysis of mimical and autonomic components of man's autonomic state. *Aviation, Space, and Environmental Medicine, 46*, 1132–1134.

Schlosberg, H. (1941). A scale for the judgment of facial expression. *Journal of Experimental Psychology*, 1941, *29*, 497–510.

Schlosberg, H. (1952). The description of facial expressions in terms of two dimensions. *Journal of Experimental Psychology*, 1952, *44*, 229–237.

Schlosberg, H. (1954). Three dimensions of emotion. *Psychological Review, 61*, 81–88.

Schwartz, G. E., Brown, S. L., & Ahern, G. L. (1980). Facial muscle patterning and subjective experience during affective imagery. *Psychophysiology, 17*, 75–82.

Schwartz, G. E., Fair, P. L., Mandel, M. R., Salt, P., Mieske, M., & Klerman, G. L. (1978). Facial electromyography in the assessment of improvement in depression. *Psychosomatic Medicine, 40*, 355–360.

Schwartz, G. E., Fair, P. L., Salt, P., Mandel, M. R., & Klerman, G. L. (1976a). Facial expression and imagery in depression: An electromyographic study. *Psychosomatic Medicine, 38*, 337–347.

Schwartz, G. E., Fair, P. L., Salt, P., Mandel, M. R., & Klerman, G. L. (1976b). Facial muscle patterning to affective imagery in depressed and nondepressed subjects. *Science, 192*, 489–491.

Sumitsuji, N., Matsumoto, K., Tanaka, M., Kashiwagi, T., & Kaneko, Z. (1967). Electromyographic investigation of the facial muscles. *Electromyography, 7*, 77–96.

Sumitsuji, N., Matsumoto, K., Tanaka, M., Kashiwagi, T., & Kaneko, Z. (1977). An attempt to systematize human emotion from EMG study of the facial expression. *Proceedings of the 4th Congress of the International College of Psychosomatic Medicine*, Kyoto, Japan.

Teasdale, J. D., & Bancroft, J. (1977). Manipulation of thought content as a determinant of mood and corrugator activity in depressed patients. *Journal of Abnormal Psychology, 86*, 235–241.

Teasdale, J. D., & Rezin, V. (1978). Effect of thought-stopping on thoughts, mood and corrugator EMG in depressed patients. *Behavior Research and Therapy, 16*, 97–102.

Vaughan, K. B., & Lanzetta, J. T. (1980). Vicarious instigation and conditioning of facial expressive and autonomic responses to a model's expressive display of pain. *Journal of Personality and Social Psychology, 38*, 909–923.

Vaughan, K. B., & Lanzetta, J. T. (1981). The effect of modulation of expressive displays on vicarious emotional arousal. *Journal of Experimental Social Psychology, 17*, 16–30.

Walbott, H. G. (1982). Audiovisual recording: procedures, equipment, and troubleshooting. In K. R. Scherer & P. Ekman (Eds.), *Handbook of methods in nonverbal behavior research* (pp. 542–579). Cambridge: Cambridge University Press.

4 VOCAL ASSESSMENT OF AFFECTIVE DISORDERS

Klaus R. Scherer
University of Geneva, Switzerland
University of Giessen, West Germany

Since antiquity, the important role of voice and speech patterns in communicating affect and affect disturbances has been frequently acknowledged. There can be no doubt that practicing clinicians regularly use the vocal sounds and speech patterns of their patients to aid them in diagnosing the type of pathology as well as shifts in mood state and long-term improvement. Even a cursory glance at psychiatry textbooks and diagnostic manuals shows that parameters of voice quality and speech are considered to be major criteria for differential diagnoses and state assessment. Many clinicians, reflecting on their work experience, readily admit to the fact that the patients' voice and speech patterns have a strong effect on their overall evaluation. However, the use of these vocal diagnostic indicators is almost always of a very intuitive nature rather than a trained skill in differentially utilizing specific voice and speech cues, let alone the use of objective measurement procedures.

Diamond (1981, p. 246–247) outlines the problem as follows:

> It is striking that in the many clinical and research descriptions of psychopathology, so little attention has been paid to the sound and enunciation of speech. Content of speech and nonverbal expression have been studied at great length and are familiar to every clinician and researcher. . . . Yet other than imprecise, vague references to tempo, such as slowing or "pressure" of speech or to observations of the incongruity of tone of voice to speech content, little acknowledgement is made to the diagnostic importance of nonlinguistic elements of communication. Even when we attempt to judge emotional expression by tone of voice, relating it to rage, depression, euphoria, or schizophrenic dissociation of affect, we rely on acoustic

> variations which are neither described nor defined in other than conclusionary manner.

This neglect is particularly apparent for the clinical study of voice quality. Although there have been quite a number of studies on the temporal and continuity aspects of speech (Goldmann-Eisler, 1968; Mahl & Schulze, 1964; Dittmann, 1972; Siegman, this volume) there has been very little work on vocal features such as pitch, intonation, or voice quality in the sense of timbre of the voice. This is all the more surprising because there have been quite a number of early investigators attempting to use electroacoustic equipment to analyze phonatory and articulatory parameters of speech in clinical populations in an objective manner (Scripture, 1921, 1927; Isserlin, 1925; Zwirner, 1930). Even though the results of these early, limited studies were quite suggestive, they have not been widely disseminated, nor has this research served as a model for other researchers in this area. Similarly, the pioneering work published by Ostwald about forty years later (Ostwald, 1963, 1964), although widely acknowledged and frequently cited, has not had an impact in the sense of either encouraging systematic empirical work in this area or leading to attempts to better define the auditory cues useful to the clinician.

The lack of work on the diagnostic utility of voice quality patterns for the assessment of affective disturbance is all the more regrettable, because one can easily show that the linkage between emotion and voice is particularly close. Thus, both neuropsychological evidence for animals (e.g. Jürgens, 1974, 1979) and humans (Robinson, 1972) shows that the limbic system structures that mediate emotion are centrally involved in the elicitation of vocalization. Furthermore, on the level of the autonomic nervous system and the somatic nervous system, there is very good evidence that changes, for example, in respiration patterns and muscle tension, have a very powerful impact on a large number of parameters of vocalization. As will be outlined below, there is also a rather high probability that the effect of the emotions on voice production is highly differentiated. At the same time, it is very important to realize that almost all of the vocal cues that are available to the listener are multiply determined. In addition to the physiologically based effects of emotional arousal on phonation and articulation, we often find expression management serving self presentation or expression control demanded by sociocultural norms. Furthermore, quite a large number of vocal cues are determined in part by the phonological and syntactic structure of a given language. Consequently, it is one of the tasks of a diagnostician to untangle the multiple determinants of the vocal cues under study.

This paper is an attempt to (a) describe the vocal parameters that seem most useful for the objective assessment of voice quality for clinical use, (b) review the literature in the area of the vocal expression of affective disturbance, and (c) propose a model for future research on the vocal assessment of affective disturbance.

SURVEY OF VOCAL PARAMETERS

Levels of Description of Vocal Behavior

Vocal behavior can be assessed at four different levels:

1. the physiological level, including description of nerve impulses, or muscle innervation patterns that form the basis for the action of the structures involved in the voice production process;
2. the phonatory-articulatory level, including description of the position and/or movement of the major structures involved, such as the vocal folds or the tongue;
3. the acoustic level, including description of characteristics of the speech waves emanating from the mouth, and
4. the subjective auditory impression a listener experiences as a result of being exposed to a vocalization.

Clearly, these levels are in some sense sequentially organized, because the lower levels precede and determine the higher levels. Thus, while it is possible to develop translation rules from one level to another (provided that the relationship is sufficiently well researched), the information obtained from these levels of description is different and may be differentially useful depending on the nature of the question asked. Given this specificity, it is of central importance to keep these levels of description apart in a measurement system. Unfortunately, quite a few of the category systems proposed for paralinguistic phenomena (Crystal, 1969, 1975; Key, 1977; Laver & Hutcheson, 1972; Poyatos, 1976; Trager, 1958) mix categories belonging to different levels of description. Apart from the methodological problems, including the definition of the parameters and the operation of their measurement, this mixture may produce severe problems in the interpretation of the findings. Below, these levels of description are discussed separately with a review of the major parameters that seem to be useful to measure at each level.

The Physiological Level

Although medical researchers in the otolaryngological area have developed a number of sophisticated methods to assess physiological processes related to phonation and articulation, many of these procedures are intrusive and do not lend themselves easily to clinical or experimental research. However, there are some methods that would seem to be within the reach of the clinical researcher and that provide important indices of the physiological processes underlying speech production. One of these is the measurement of respiration. Strain gauges or thermistors can be used to assess both depth and rate of respiration, both of which strongly affect phonation. Furthermore, surface EMG (electromyography) can be used to assess the overall tone of the muscle region around the larynx and in the lower face region. Although such measurements are obviously undifferentiated, they may be useful to assess the level of system tension. While researchers in physiological phonetics have used needle electrodes to probe the activity of individual muscles involved in the phonation and articulation process, these methods are unlikely to be useful with patients or volunteer subjects.

A further variable of the physiological level, which may be useful to assess the activity of the parasympathetic system, is the measurement of salivation, for example, in psychopharmacology experiments, using the weighing of intraoral cotton swabs before and after drug application. Salivation changes the resonance characteristics of the vocal tract and, in connection with mucus secretion, the activity of the vocal folds. Changes in salivation may thus have noticeable effects on phonation and resonance.

The variables discussed can be expected to have a direct influence on voice and speech production. Further physiological measurements may be more indirectly related to vocalization patterns. Future research may show, for example, lawful relationships between heart-rate measures and voice production phenomena. Given the scarcity of appropriate studies, at present we know very little about the relationships between physiological parameters and voice production processes.

The Phonatory-Articulatory Level

On the phonatory-articulation level, measurement involves the assessment of the actual movement, in terms of location, trajectory, and speed of the various phonatory and articulatory mechanisms, such as the vocal folds, the velum, and the tongue. Scherer (1982) provides a short primer of voice production processes. Again, physiological phoneticians have developed advanced technologies, involving high-speed photography, transducer measurements, and electronic contact measurement to assess changes in the phonatory and articulatory structures occurring during voicing and speech. However, as with the advanced physiological methods, many of these procedures are not practical for studies with patients or large numbers of naive volunteer subjects. Because many of these moving structures are not directly visible, observational methods are unlikely to be useful. The exception is movement of the musculature in the lower face region producing phenomena such as lip rounding, jaw protrusion, or tensing of the orbicularis oris muscle. The method of choice for the systematic assessment of these articulatory structures could be a specially-adapted version of Ekman and Friesen's Facial Action Coding System (see Ekman & Fridlund, this volume).

For trained phoneticians and possibly experienced coders trained by such phoneticians, it is possible to infer the phonatory and articulatory structures from the characteristics of the acoustic sound wave. A coding system for a variety of stable vocal settings, that is, particular configurations of the vocal tract and vocal fold activity for vocalizations of longer duration, has been developed by John Laver and his associates at the University of Edinburgh. Table 4.1 shows the categories in this classification scheme. The system has been taught to a number of coders and has been used mainly in research on voice pathology. However, this general approach is useful in a variety of clinical approaches, particularly for

TABLE 4.1
Summary Listing of the Categories Proposed by Laver for the Phonatory-Articulatory Description of Voice Quality

Supralaryngeal settings		*Laryngeal settings*
Longitudinal axis settings:		*Simple phonation types:*
Labial	Labial protrusion	Modal voice
	Labiodentalization	Falsetto
Laryngeal	Raised larynx	Whisper
	Lowered larynx	Creak
Latitudinal axis settings:		*Compound phonation types:*
Labial	Close rounding	Whispery voice
	Open rounding	Whispery falsetto
	Lip-spreading	Creaky voice
Lingual		Creaky falsetto
Tip/blade	Tip articulation	Whispery creak
	Blade articulation	Whispery creaky voice
	Retroflex articulation	Whispery creaky falsetto
Tongue-body	Dentalized	Breathy voice
	Palato-alveolarized	Harsh voice
	Palatalized	Harsh falsetto
	Velarized	Harsh whispery voice
	Pharyngalized	Harsh whispery falsetto
	Laryngopharyngalized	Harsh creaky voice
Mandibular	Close jaw position	Harsh creaky falsetto
	Open jaw position	Harsh whispery creaky voice
	Protruded jaw position	Harsh whispery creaky falsetto
	Retracted jaw position	
Velopharyngeal settings:		*Overall muscular tension settings:*
	Nasal	Tense voice
	Denasal	Lax voice

Note: Laver and Hanson, 1981, p. 70. By permission of Grune & Stratton.

the measurement of affect and affect disturbances as revealed by voice quality characteristics.

The Acoustic Level

Although some of the measurement on the preceding two levels may be useful for a number of specialized research applications, the most widely applicable level for objective measurement is the acoustic one. All that is required for sophisticated sets of measurement in this domain are reasonably good quality tape recordings of a speaker's voice, preferably for an utterance of at least several words. Using relatively simple analog electroacoustic devices such as oscillographs or amplitude meters, pitch meters or frequency spectrum analyzers, or all purpose digital speech analyzers, a number of acoustic parameters can be extracted from the speech signal contained on the tape. These acoustic parameters have been shown to be highly relevant to the diagnosis of emotion and affect disturbance.

The available space does not permit detailed description of these parameters and their assessment. Scherer (1982) introduces some of the basic concepts in speech acoustics. Table 4.2 shows a list of the acoustic parameters that can potentially be extracted from the acoustic speech signal. Items in Table 4.2 have been shown in past research (or can be demonstrated theoretically) to have an important function in the expression of emotion and affective disorders. Scherer (1982) describes the methods for measuring these variables in somewhat more detail as well as providing some indication of the evidence to date concerning the diagnostic validity of these parameters.

As will be discussed later, a large number of these parameters have been shown to differentiate various patient groups as well as to be centrally related to the severity of the disturbance or improvement over therapy. In addition, there is a strong likelihood that pharmacologically-induced changes can be monitored by the use of some of these voice parameters. Consequently, these methods and parameters promise to be of major importance for clinical research and practice.

Apart from the machine analysis of acoustic phenomena, there is a possibility of using trained raters to assess at least some of the acoustic parameters such as loudness, pitch, intonation contour change, and some voice quality parameters. However, although such auditory assessments are correlated with the underlying acoustic variables, the relationship is far from perfect. The filtering and integration characteristics of the human auditory system render it difficult to analytically separate a number of acoustic parameters. Thus, many of the auditory ratings in the acoustic domain are conglomerates of several different acoustic cues. Needless to say, this may lead to serious problems in the interpretation of the ratings. Furthermore, few attempts have been made to develop a category svstem or training tapes that would allow assessment of the validity and reliability of such an auditory acoustic rating system.

TABLE 4.2
Overview of Major Acoustic Parameters

Parameter	*Description*
F0 perturbation	Slight variations in the duration of glottal cycles
F0 mean	Fundamental frequency (vibration rate of vocal folds as averaged over a speech utterance)
F0 range	Difference between highest and lowest F0 in an utterance
F0 variability	Measure of dispersion (e.g., standard deviation of F0)
F0 contour	Fundamental frequency values plotted over time (intonation)
F1 mean	Frequency of the first (lowest) formant (significant energy concentration in the spectrum) averaged over an utterance
F2 mean	Mean frequency of the second formant
Formant bandwidth	Width of the spectral band containing significant formant energy
Formant precision	Degree to which formant frequencies attain values prescribed by phonological system of a language
Intensity mean	Energy values for a speech sound wave averaged over an utterance
Intensity range	Difference between highest and lowest intensity values in an utterance
Intensity variability	Measure of dispersion of intensity values in an utterance (e.g., standard deviation)
Frequency range	Difference between F0 and highest point in the frequency spectrum where there is still speech energy
High-frequency energy	Relative proportion of energy in the upper frequency region (e.g., > 1 kHz)
Spectral noise	Aperiodic energy components in the spectrum
Speech rate	Number of speech segments per time unit

Note. F0 = fundamental frequency. F1 = first formant. F2 = second formant.
Note. Reproduced from Scherer, 1986a, p. 149. By permission of the American Psychological Association.

The Subjective Impression Level

In many ways the subjective impression level is not a proper description for the characteristics of the voice and speech output of a speaker. However, it can provide interesting insights into the signaling functions and expressive characteristics of vocalizations. The assessment procedure simply consists in asking naive judges to rate speech samples on widely-used natural language labels for voice and speech characteristics. Table 4.3 shows a factor analysis of a number of such widely used adjectives. An attempt to reduce the large number of appropriate adjectives to the major dimensions (which are found repeatedly in analyses of this kind) is currently in progress.

TABLE 4.3
Scales for Ratings of Proximal Vocal Cues for Voice Quality and Speech Characteristics

Voice Quality		*Speech Characteristics*	
1. *Pleasantness*	8. *Sharpness*	1 *Precision*	4. *Rhythm*
Clear	Ringing	Fluent	Rhythmic
Cultured	Sharp	Distinct	Accentuated
Melodic	9. *Loudness*	Poised	Cadenced
Expressive	Loud	Clear	Accented
Flexible	Penetrating	Articulated	5. *Affectation*
Pleasant	10. *Harshness*	Precise	Pathetic
2. *Resonance*	Harsh	Exact	Mannered
Masculine	Rough	Controlled	Crawling
Strong	11 *Gloom*	Meticulous	Affected
Resonant	Gloomy	2. *Rate*	6. *Regularity*
Sonorous	Muffled	Fast	Calm
3. *Depth*	12. *Hoarseness*	Clipped	Regular
Dark	Hoarse	Hasty	Uniform
Deep	Throaty	Hurried	
4. *Breathiness*	13. *Flatness*	3. *Sloppiness*	
Breathy	Flat	Fuzzy	
Broken	14. *Nasality*	Monotonous	
Quavering	Nasal	Slurred	
5. *Warmth*	15. *Dryness*	Jerky	
Mellow	Dry	Sloppy	
Soothing			
Warm			
6. *Thinness*			
Effeminate			
Thin			
7 *High-pitch*			
High-pitched			
Light			

Note. Based on voice- and speech-attribute rating forms developed by K. R. Scherer (1970). The clusters proposed here result from factor analyses of American and German rater groups, including self-, peer, and stranger ratings. *Source:* Scherer, 1982, p. 173. By permission of Cambridge University Press.

VOCAL INDICATORS OF AFFECTIVE DISTURBANCE: A REVIEW OF THE LITERATURE

The present state of the art in this field is reasonably well captured by the studies listed in Table 4.4 (see also Darby, 1981). This table represents, as one might say, the scraping of the barrel. As will be readily noted, a large number of these studies do not meet the minimal requirements for serious empirical research. Consequently, the results and many of the conclusions drawn, are offered with reservation, motivated only by the feeling that even anecdotal, case history, or very weak quantitative data may help to further the process of hypothesis generation and may stimulate the launching of well controlled clinical research.

Methodological Issues

Clearly, the special contingencies of clinical settings constrain the possibilities for rigorous experimental design, and the availability of appropriate subject populations often hampers progress even when appropriate research designs exist. As Table 4.4 shows, many of the studies listed have used very few patients, in some cases only one, to draw conclusions as to the vocal cues indicative of depression. It is likely that such studies have been accepted by journal editors and book publishers because the conclusions seemed in line with the general stereotype concerning the depressive voice. Yet, as we shall see, the pattern of findings is hardly as clear-cut as one might hope for before closing the issue.

Table 4.4 lists the authors and the year of the study in the first column, and the number, sex, and gross diagnosis of the patients studied in the second column. The latter, as will be readily apparent, is very problematic indeed. In many studies, little additional specification other than that of "depression" is given as far as a specific diagnosis is concerned. Although a few studies are notable exceptions in that a rather detailed diagnostic background is provided, one is generally forced to speculate about what type of patient may have been studied in a particular case. This problem is all the more serious because the terminology in the past 50 years has hardly been uniform as far as the nosological categories for depression are concerned. Furthermore, most of the studies report aggregate data for groups of patients or across several assessment points in time. Given that affectively disturbed persons rarely remain in the same state over many periods of time, particularly because bipolar syndromes tend to produce rather marked changes, comparison of data within and across studies is very difficult indeed.

Quite apart from these problems, there are a number of additional sources for incompatibility due to differences in methodology. In the column labelled "Aim" in Table 4.4, it is noted whether the study originally aimed at a mere description of the vocal characteristics of depressive patients (symptom description: SD), differential diagnosis either in comparison with other psychiatric groups or in comparison with normal subjects (DD), state changes in terms of different phases of affect disturbance state (SC), or change during therapy (CT), trying to establish the effectiveness of therapeutic intervention on the basis of vocal indicators. Given the diversity of these research aims, it is not surprising that both the type of methodology used to obtain the stimulus material and the nature of the data analysis is rather different.

In the next column of Table 4.4 the type of speech sample used is described. The two basic methods that have been used in this area to obtain utterances for analysis are the use of free responses in interviews (either standardized or non-

TABLE 4.4
Summary of Studies on Vocal Indicators of Depression

No.	*Study*	*Subjects*	*Aim*	*Utt*	*Inst*	*Brief Summary of Major Findings*
1	Zwimer, 1930	1 f dep	SD	IR	EE	repeated downward FO contours
2*	Newman & Mather, 1938	40 mixed dep	DD	IR	RJ	
		a) classic dep				a) narrow pitch range, rare pitch changes, slow tempo, many pauses, weak accents, pharyngeal & nasal resonance, listless voice quality
		b) dissatis/gloom				b) wide tonal range, long gliding intonation, crisp articulation, lively voice, frequent pauses, glottal rasp
		c) manic				c) wide pitch range, frequent gliding pitch changes, emphatic accent, rhythmic pauses exaggerated in length, clear vital voice, oral & pharyngeal resonance, short latency, vigorous articulation
3	Moses, 1954	1 m dep	SD	IR	RJ	repeated downward pitch contour, low intensity, low pitch
4	Zuberbier, 1957	20 f dep, 20 matched norm	DD	RT	EE	reduced intensity, narrow FO range, stepwise FO changes, level pitch contours (lack of final sentence FO drop), reduced dynamic range, lack of emphatic accent, lax and slow articulation, increase in number & length of pauses
5	Eldred & Price, 1958	1 f dep	SD	IR	RJ	decrease in pitch level, tempo & intensity in depressive phases
6	Ostwald, 1961	1 m dep	CT	IR	EE	intensity increase, particularly around 500 Hz
7	Ostwald, 1963	a) 1 f, 7 m dep	SD	IR	EE	a) flat & hollow voice quality as defined by spectral parameters
		b) 17 f, 13 m mixed	CT	RT	EE	b) intensity changes after ECT
8	Ostwald, 1964	1 f dep	SD	IR	EE	lack of FO variation, flat voice
9	Hargreaves & Starkweather, 1964	8 mixed dep	CT	IR	EE	intensity increase, partic. in higher formants, for some patients
10	Hargreaves et al., 1965	23 f, 9 m dep	CT	IR	EE	reduced intensity, partic. in high overtones, reduced inflection, dull, lifeless voice, for some patients

11	Hargreaves & Starkweather, 1965	4 f dep	CT	IR	EE	FO, intensity, tempo increase for 3 retarded patients, no change for agitated patient
12*	Whitman & Flicker, 1966	1f, 2m mixed	SC	RT	EE	increased FO level & reduction in intensity with greater severity; greater tempo in agitated patient
13*	Bannister, 1972	45 mixed adolesc., 45 norm	DD	RT	EE	lower levels FO in females, reduced FO range
14*	Harlan, 1974	21 m, 21 f mixed	DD	RT	RJ	frequent voice disorders, abnormal intonation, more pitch breaks in manic patients
15	Roessler & Lester, 1976	1 f dep	SC	IR	DA	decreased FO in depressive phases, increased FO in anxiety phases
16	Darby & Hollien, 1977	4 f, 2 m dep	CT	RT	RJ	ratings show improvement in articulation, inflection, stress; less dull voice, voice quality & more vitality after therapy, acoustic variables show no change
17*	Denber, 1978	61 m dep, 20 m schiz, 31 m norm	DD	RT	DA	differences in voice spectrum between normals and patients, diff in jitter between dep and schiz
18	Askenfelt & Sjölin, 1980	a) 4 dep, 4 norm	DD	RT	DA	a) no difference to normals but greater frequency variation after sleep deprivation
		b) 3 dep	CT	RT	DA	b) increase in FO rate of change
19*	Fleischmenn, 1980	11 dep, 2 schiz, 3 norm	DD	?	DA	greater FO standard deviation in depressives
20	Heitman, 1980	2 m, 2 f dep 4 m, 4 f schiz	DD SC	IR	DA	higher FO variability in manic & agitated phases, generally higher FO variability in positive mood states
21*	Jimenez, 1981	8 dep, 10 norm	DD	?	DA	longer phoneme duration
22	Tolkmitt et al., 1982	17 f dep, 15 f schiz	CT DD	IR	DA	decrease in FO, increase of intensity in low frequency band, change of formant frequencies in direction of more precise articulation, for depressives; inconclusive results for schiz.
23	Bildhauer, 1985	11 f, 5 m dep	SC	IR	DA	FO floor decrease for subjectively more positive mood states
24*	Darby et al., 1984	15 dep	CT	RT	RJ	changes in stress, pitch, loudness after drug treatment

Abbreviations: *cited after secondary source; m = male, f = female; dep = depressive, schiz = schizophrenic, norm = normal; SD = symptom description, DD = differential diagnosis, SC = state change, CT = change after therapy; IR = interview responses, RT = reading text;

standardized interviews or the reading or recitation of a standard text. Again, the differences between these two types of speech sample elicitation are pronounced. It is well known, for example, that the fundamental frequency of the voice tends to be generally higher in reading compared to free speech. Furthermore, the content of interview material is likely to be much more ego-involved and affectively charged than the reading materials that are often nonsensical or irrelevant. An additional problem is that reading probably more than an interview situation might be considered as an achievement task which induces a stress response in the patient. Consequently, it is not obvious that one can easily compare findings from studies using different voice elicitation techniques.

A final problem in using vocal indicators of affective disturbances is due to the nature of the analysis procedures chosen. In quite a number of studies listed in Table 4.4, raters, usually experts in phonetics or speech pathology, have been used to assess voice and speech characteristics. In other studies, particularly recent ones, either electroacoustic equipment such as fundamental frequency meters, amplitude meters, or spectroanalyzers, or digital speech analysis on minicomputers have been used for voice analysis. Although there is, as mentioned above, a lawful relationship between the auditory impression of basic acoustic variables and the objective measures of these variables, the relationship is far from perfect and may vary with the nature of the speech sample and the kind of raters used. For example, in assessing pitch and pitch range, raters are strongly affected by differences in the energy distribution in the spectrum. Again, these differences in the instruments chosen make it very difficult to compare the findings in a reasonable fashion.

Voice Intensity

Given all these caveats, what are the preliminary conclusions that one might want to draw from the pattern of results (and speculations) shown in Table 4.4? The most consistent finding is that depressives seem to speak with rather low intensity (studies 3, 4, 5, 12 in Table 4.4) and that intensity generally seems to increase after therapy (studies 6, 7, 9, 11, 22 in Table 4.4). Although some studies seem to indicate that the increase of energy is mainly due to greater energy in the lower frequencies up to about 500 or 1000 Hz (studies 6,7), at least one study (9) points towards an increase of energy in the higher overtones. Generally, however, there seems to be rather strong agreement on the low intensity of depressive voices and in the one study that has assessed this variable, a low dynamic range, that is, a rather narrow band of intensity changes (study 4) is reported.

Fundamental Frequency of the Voice

Such agreement is missing in the area of fundamental frequency (FO) of the voice (see Table 4.2). While a number of studies seem to indicate that depressive voices have a rather low FO mean or floor (studies 3, 5, 13, 15 in Table 4.4), one study finds an increase in FO with the severity of depression (study 12 in Table

4.4). Similarly, a number of studies find a rather narrow range and restricted variability for FO in depressive speech (studies 2, 4, 8, 10, 13 in Table 4.4) whereas others tend to find wide FO range in variability in certain depressive patients (studies 2, 19, 20). Mirroring this difference, some studies on changes after therapy find a decrease in FO after therapy or during positive mood (studies 22, 23), whereas another implies a possible increase (study 11). Only one study has looked at changes in FO variability (study 18) and finds an increase after therapy. It should be noted that at least some of the studies that find wide FO range do so only for subgroups of patients that are either in a manic or an agitated (studies 2, 20) state.

It is highly likely that the inconsistency that seems to exist in the data is due to the major problem of patient symptom homogeneity mentioned above. It is quite possible that depressive patients with strong components of anxiety or patients in manic phases of a bipolar illness, can be expected to show high FO and wide FO range. Patients during depressive phases or in a retarded category, on the other hand, would be likely to manifest low FO and very narrow FO range. Depending on the nature of the diagnostic group, one would expect very different FO parameters during the illness and different changes following therapeutic improvement. Although this interpretation would have to be checked carefully, it seems obvious that more refined differential diagnosis of patient subgroups is needed when investigating possible vocal indicators of affective disorder.

Most studies have focused on intensity and fundamental frequency. Fewer studies have investigated some of the other acoustic parameters that have been listed in Table 4.2. Consequently, it is almost impossible to draw any inferences from the available data. In the following, I will describe some interesting hypotheses suggested by some of the results.

For example, many clinicians have commented on the fact that depressive speech often sounds monotonous. Some studies (1, 2, 3 in Table 4.4) remark that many of the patients' utterances seem to use rather stereotypical downward-directed intonation contours that are repeated frequently. It could be that the impression of monotonousness is linked primarily to the fact that there is little variety in the form of the intonation contour rather than to the flatness of the contour.

On the other hand, Zuberbier (1957) argued that depressive inflection often seems to lack the characteristic fall of the FO contour at the end of a sentence, remaining rather flat throughout. This is a very interesting point for further investigation, particularly in so far as it addresses the issue of the relationship between objective acoustic characteristics that can be used in a diagnostic fashion and the nature of the listener interpretation which, of course, plays a major role in the patient's interaction with the social world.

Articulation

A parameter that is of particular interest, given the potentially important role of muscle tension, is precision of articulation. There is some indication that depressives speak with rather lax articulation, and that articulation preciseness increases after therapy (studies 4, 22 in Table 4.4). Imprecise articulation, that is, the failure of the articulatory organs to reach their targets, could be due to both hypotension and hypertension (in which case one would expect problems of coordination in moving the articulators). It may be necessary to complement the assessment of vocal cues of depression with other assessments of muscle tension such as EMG measurement.

Speech Characteristics

Another major domain that seems clearly related to the characteristics of depressive speech are speech rate or tempo and pauses as well as emphatic accent. As in the case of FO and FO range, we find apparently contradictory results. Some studies find slow tempo, many pauses, and weak emphatic accents for patients (2, 4, 5 in Table 4.4), whereas others report the opposite (2, 12). As before, this discrepancy is easily resolved if one realizes that the studies finding a fast tempo and strong accenting pattern do so only for manic or agitated depressive patients (2, 12). It is clear that the speech patterns in retarded and agitated, or depressed and manic patients are different, indeed almost opposite in terms of their characteristics. This, of course, does not come as a surprise to clinicians. Unfortunately, research in this area has not consistently differentiated the different syndromes and the different phases in a manic-depressive cycle. Further progress in this area strongly demands a much more careful and consistent diagnostic grouping of the patient population before studies of vocal indicators of depression are undertaken.

However, not all of the problems with data in consistency are due to the lack of homogeneity in diagnostic subgroups. One of the major difficulties in interpreting FO, for example, is that this value is not independent of the intensity of vocal effort of speech. Although we can vary both of these parameters independently by voluntary action, there seems to be some inherent coupling resulting in the reduction of FO with a fall in intensity or vocal effort. Thus, if intensity is reduced for many depressive patients (as many studies seem to indicate), this would, by necessity entail a change in FO. Because both intensity and FO are dependent on the activity of a large number of different structures and can be changed in many different ways, the issue is a highly complex one.

A THEORETICAL MODEL FOR RESEARCH ON VOCAL CUES OF AFFECTIVE DISORDERS

The preceding review shows that the evidence at present is inconclusive. There can be little doubt that the intuitive feeling that voice is an important indicator of affect state (shared by clinicians and researchers alike) is supported by the data.

However, the nature of the relationship between specific affect states and affect disturbances on the one hand and various voice and speech characteristics on the other hand is hardly known. It is not likely that the problem lies with the inconsistency or the absence of strong relationships. Even a cursory review of the studies shows, the major reason for the sad state of the art is the lack of well-controlled empirical studies that use appropriately large groups of homogeneous patient and control populations, appropriate voice and speech sampling, and established acoustic parameters and measurement. Many of the studies reviewed above are deficient on one or several of these counts. However, even worse than the obvious inadequacies of the studies reported in the literature, is the lack of a theoretical model that allows specification of the mechanism for vocal changes following emotional arousal or affect disturbance.

Theoretical Model of Emotion

This situation is comparable to the research area concerned with the vocal expression of normal emotion. In an attempt to overcome the problems of an exclusively atheoretical approach to vocal affect analysis, the author has proposed (Scherer, 1986a; in prep.) a component patterning model of vocal affect expression based on a new theory of emotion, the component process model of emotion (Scherer, 1981, 1984). In this approach, emotion is seen as a process consisting of changes in the states of several organismic subsystems, that is, components of emotion such as information processing, physiological arousal, expression, action tendencies, and subjective feeling.

The differentiation of the various emotional states is produced by the results of a series of "stimulus evaluation checks" that help the organism to evaluate the significance of external and internal stimuli. Table 4.5 lists those stimulus evaluation checks and their subchecks. It is argued that the organism constantly scans the environment and processes significant stimuli by evaluating them against the criteria in the various checks. The results of specific checks can lead to particular emotions. For example, a novel event is likely to produce surprise. In most cases, however, complex emotions such as anger are produced by the results of several of these checks. For example, I would expect that hot anger or rage is produced by novel stimuli that are highly relevant to the organism, but discrepant from expectation and obstructive to the organism's goal. Furthermore, rage-producing stimuli require urgent action in a situation characterized by high control of the organism over outcomes and a high degree of power to influence these outcomes. The outcomes on the pleasantness and goal-need conduciveness checks in an evaluation process leading to rage can be very similar to comparable outcomes in fear situations. However, whatever control possibilities there are, fear situations are characterized by low power, which makes flight or submission the only possible alternative. A detailed prediction table for the respective out-

TABLE 4.5
Description of Stimulus Evaluation Checks (SECs)

1. *Novelty check.* Evaluating whether there is a change in the pattern of external or internal stimulation, particularly whether a novel event occurred or is to be expected.
2. *Intrinsic pleasantness check.* Evaluating whether a stimulus event is pleasant, inducing approach tendencies, or unpleasant, inducing avoidance tendencies; based on innate feature detectors or on learned associations.
3. *Goal/need significance check.* Evaluating whether a stimulus event is relevant to important goals or needs of the organism (relevance subcheck), whether the outcome is consistent with or discrepant from the state expected for this point in the goal/plan sequence (expectation subcheck), whether it is conducive or obstructive to reaching the respective goals or satisfying the relevant needs (conduciveness check), and how urgently some kind of behavioral response is required (urgency subcheck).
4. *Coping potential check.* Evaluating the causation of a stimulus event (causation subcheck) and the coping potential available to the organism, particularly the degree of control over the event or its consequences (control subcheck), the relative power of the organism to change or avoid the outcome through fight or flight (power subcheck), and the potential for adjustment to the final outcome via internal restructuring (adjustment subcheck).
5. *Norm/self compatibility check.* Evaluating whether the event, particularly an action, conforms to social norms, cultural conventions, or expectations of significant others (external standards subcheck), and whether it is consistent with internalized norms or standards as part of the self-concept or ideal self (internal standards subcheck).

Note. **Reproduced from Scherer, 1986a, p. 147. By permission of the American Psychological Association.**

comes of the various stimulus evaluation checks for a set of major emotions is shown in Table 4.6.

The componential patterning model postulates that each of the respective outcomes on the sequence of checks differentially affects the various subsystems of the organism (components of emotion) and produces a characteristic set of changes. For example, a stimulus evaluated as novel will produce an orienting response; a stimulus that is very significant, obstructive to a goal, and requiring urgent action, can be expected to produce a major increase in sympathetic arousal (see Scherer, 1984; 1986a; in prep., for a more detailed description of the model).

In terms of the voice response to the various outcomes of the SECs, detailed predictions have been developed. These predictions, both in terms of the phonatory-articulatory phenomena and their acoustic consequences are shown in Table 4.7. Elsewhere (Scherer, 1986a), I have shown how these predictions can be used to develop specific hypotheses about the acoustic cues that should allow differentiation of various normal emotions.

The approach suggested here aims at providing the missing link between underlying psychological processes, their physiological correlates, and the effect

TABLE 4.6
Hypothetical Outcomes of Stimulus Evaluation Checks for Selected Emotional States

			Goal/Need Significance				Coping Potential			Norm Compatibility	
Emotional State	*Novelty*	*Pleasantness*	*Relevance*	*Expectation*	*Conduciveness*	*Urgency*	*Control*	*Power*	*Adjust*	*External*	*Internal*
Enjoyment/happiness	Low	High	Medium	Consistent	High	Very low	—	—	High	High	High
Elation/joy	High	High	High	Discrepant	High	Low	—	—	Medium	High	High
Displeasure/disgust	Open	Very low	Low	Discrepant	Low	Medium	Open	Open	High	Low	—
Contempt/scorn	Open	Low	Low	Discrepant	Low	Low	Open	High	High	Low	—
Sadness/dejection	Low	Low	High	Discrepant	Obstruct	Low	None	—	Medium	—	—
Grief/desperation	High	Low	High	Discrepant	Obstruct	High	Low	Low	Low	—	—
Anxiety/worry	Low	Open	Medium	Discrepant	Obstruct	Medium	Open	Low	Medium	—	—
Fear/terror	High	Low	High	Discrepant	Obstruct	Very high	Open	Very low	Medium	—	—
Irritation/cold anger	Low	Open	Medium	Discrepant	Obstruct	Medium	High	Medium	High	Low	Low
Rage/hot anger	High	Open	High	Discrepant	Obstruct	High	High	High	High	Low	Low
Boredom/indifference	Very low	Open	Low	Consistent	Obstruct	Low	Medium	Medium	High	—	—
Shame/guilt	Low	Open	High	Discrepant	Obstruct	Medium	High	Open	Medium	Very low	Very low

Note. Reproduced from Scherer, 1986a, p. 147. By permission of the American Psychological Association.

TABLE 4.7
Component Patterning Theory Predictions of Vocal Changes After Different SEC Outcomes

Novelty check	
Novel	*Old*
Interruption of phonation Sudden inhalation Silence Ingressive (fricative) sound with a glottal stop (noise-like spectrum)	No change
Intrinsic Pleasantness check	
Pleasant	*Unpleasant*
Faucal and pharyngeal expansion, relaxation of tract walls. Vocal tract shortened by mouth, corners retracted upward	Faucal and pharyngeal constriction, tensing of tract walls. Vocal tract shortened by mouth, corners retracted downward
More low-frequency energy, F1 falling, slightly broader F1 bandwidth, velopharyngeal nasality Resonances raised	More high-frequency energy, F1 rising, F2 and F3 falling, narrow F1 bandwidth, laryngopharyngeal nasality
Wide voice	*Narrow voice*
Goal/need significance check	
Relevant and consistent	*Relevant and discrepant*
Shift toward trophotropic side: overall relaxation of vocal apparatus, increased salivation	Ergotropic dominance: overall tensing of vocal apparatus and respiratory system, decreased salivation
F0 at lower end of range, low-to-moderate amplitude, balanced resonance with slight decrease in high-frequency energy	F0 and amplitude increase, jitter and shimmer, increase in high-frequency energy, narrow F1 bandwidth, pronounced formant frequency differences
Relaxed voice If event conducive to goal: relaxed voice + wide voice If event obstructive to goal: relaxed voice + narrow voice	*Tense voice* If event conducive to goal: tense voice + wide voice If event obstructive to goal: tense voice + narrow voice

(*Continued*)

TABLE 4.7 (*Continued*)

Coping potential check	
Control	*No control*
Ergotropic dominance: (See tense voice)	Trophotropic dominance: Hypotension of the musculature in the vocal apparatus and respiratory system
(See tense voice)	Low F0 and restricted F0 range, low-amplitude, weak pulses, very low high-frequency energy, spectral noise, formant frequencies tending toward neutral setting, broad F1 bandwidth
Tense voice	*Lax voice*
Power	*No power*
Deep, forceful respiration; chest register phonation	Rapid, shallow respiration; head register phonation
Low F0, high-amplitude, strong energy in entire frequency range	Raised F0, widely spaced harmonics with relatively low energy
Full voice	*Thin voice*
Norm/self compatibility check	
Standards surpassed	*Standard violated*
Wide voice + full voice	Narrow voice + thin voice
+ Relaxed voice (if expected)	+ Lax voice (if no control)
+ Tense voice (if unexpected)	+ Tense voice (if control)

Note. Reproduced from Scherer, 1986a, p. 156. By permission of the American Psychological Association.

of these on phonatory-articulatory events and their acoustic consequences. It is felt that even a preliminary understanding of the interrelationships between these different levels may allow us to focus empirical research and to achieve some accumulation of findings.

Role of Affective Disorders in the Model

To what extent is the component process theory of emotion and the componential patterning model suggested by it applicable to affect disturbance? I have suggested elsewhere (Scherer, 1986b) that the model can be used to conceptualize disturbed affect states. For example, stress can be defined as an emotion process characterized by either abnormal intensity or abnormal duration of an emotional episode. Under stress, emotional arousal often does not return to baseline after a fairly short period of time as would be the case with most normal emotion episodes. This link of stress with general emotion theory differentiates different types of stress depending on the underlying emotion.

Similarly, one could argue that affect disturbances can be explained by the model in terms of "abnormal" results of the various stimulus evaluation checks. Such results could lead to emotional states that are inappropriate in view of the nature of the experienced event or a person's general life situation. Inappropriate results of the stimulus evaluation checks are likely to be due, at least in part, to either misattributions in terms of the causation and significance of an event or to incorrect criteria as used in the checks, as for example, relationship to one's goals or one's degree of power or control over outside events. For example, an unrealistically low level of self esteem and coping ability is likely to produce feelings of anxiety or depression that are regarded as inappropriate or "abnormal" by other people.

Proceeding in this manner, one can take each of the checks in turn and attempt to describe the consequences of a malfunctioning of the checking process due to incorrect criteria or to deficiencies in the underlying structures. Space is not sufficient here to discuss the possible origin of such disturbances of the checking process; given that these checks can be conducted on different levels of the central nervous system (from brain stem over limbic system to cortex), one can envisage many different sources for malfunctioning from biological changes to maladaptive behavior patterns, learning experiences, or environmental influence.

As far as the intrinsic pleasantness check is concerned, a state of *anhedonia* refers to a malfunctioning of this check in that even intrinsically pleasant stimuli are no longer experienced as such. Conversely, the state of *euphoria* may be taken to refer to cases where the pleasant experience derived from a stimulus event seems to be in excess of what others might feel.

A maladaptive functioning of the goal significance check can be conceptualized in the sense of a person habitually finding that the present state of affairs is discrepant with goal/need expectations or obstructive in reaching one's goals. This discrepancy may produce a state of habitual *dissatisfaction,* frustration, and complaining. On the other hand, indifference or *apathy* might be a description for the state in which a person no longer seems capable of evaluating situations in terms of their relevance and conduciveness to important needs or goals.

One of the most important checks, particularly for depressive disorders is the coping ability check. A large number of theorists have pointed to the central factor of feelings of control and power, either from a cognitive attribution or an experience-learning point of view or both (e.g., Beck, 1967; Seligman, 1975). The predictions made on the basis of the component process theory are directly compatible with most of these approaches, although theory demands a strict separation of the subchecks of control and power. The control check refers to the possibility that events or their consequences are controllable by human agency, independent of the ability of the attributing person. No control is possible in cases where natural forces or chance are the sole determinants of an event. Power, on the other hand, refers to a person's own ability (in terms of physical might, possession of resources, problem-solving ability, information or knowledge, or ability to solicit help) to influence an event or its consequences (presuming that it is controllable). The habitual tendency to attribute uncontrollable causes to events would lead to a feeling of hopelessness. Similarly, a tendency to habitually underrate one's personal power to influence events is likely to produce helplessness.

Using these two subchecks of the model, one could postulate in a very gross way four types of inappropriate affect states:

mania	overestimation of control and power
anxiety disorders	concern about adequacy of power, but feeling that control is possible
hopelessness	underestimation of control
helplessness	underestimation of power

As would be predicted by the model, a state of ergotropic arousal is likely to be present in the first two cases and one of trophotropic arousal in the last two. It is possible that ergotropic arousal is further increased by the overestimation of the urgency of action subcheck leading to agitation.

Predicting Vocal Cues of Affective Disorder

In terms of the search for vocal indicators of affect disturbances, this rough model of affect disturbance derived from my component process model of emotion may help develop preliminary predictions that could be tested empirically in a more stringent manner than has been possible in the atheoretical research published to date. Table 4.8 shows a prediction table for voice types which is

TABLE 4.8
Voice Type Prediction for Specific Types of Affect Disorders (derived from Tables 4.5 and 4.6)

	Pharynx Setting	*Vocal Tract Tension*	*Register*
Euphoria	Wide	Medium tense	Slightly full
Mania	Wide	Extremely tense	Extremely full
Anhedonia	Very narrow	Slightly tense	Neutral
Helplessness	Narrow	Lax	Thin
Anxiety disorder	Narrow	Medium to highly tense	Thin
Agitated fear	Narrow	Extremely tense	Very thin
Chronic dissatisfaction, frustration	Narrow	Medium tense	Medium full
Indifference, apathy	Neutral	Slightly lax	Neutral
Shame, guilt	Narrow	Slightly tense	Thin

TABLE 4.9
Differences Predicted for Selected Acoustic Parameters in Comparing Voices of Normal and Affectively Disturbed Speakers (Based on the Voice Type Prediction in Table 4.4)

	Euphoria	*Mania*	*Anhedonia*	*Help-lessness*	*Anxiety Disorder*	*Agit. Fear*	*Dissatis Frust*	*Indiff Apathy*	*Shame Guilt*
F0 Perturbation				>	>	>			
F0 Mean	>			><	>	>>	><	<	>
F0 Range	>	>>	<	<	>	>>	<		
F0 Variability	>	>>	<	<	>	>>	<		
F0 Contour	>	>		<	>	>>	<		>
F1 Mean	<	<	>	>	>	>	>	>	>
F2 Mean			<	<	<	<	<	<	<
F1 Bandwidth	><	><	<	><	<<	<<	<<	<	<
Formant precision		>		<	>	>	>		>
Intensity mean	>	>>		<<	>	>	>	><	
Intensity range	>	>		<		>	>		
Intensity variability	>	>		<		>			
Frequency range	>	>>		>	>	>>	>	>	
High-frequency energy	><	><	>	><	>	>>	>	><	>
Spectral noise				>					
Speech rate	>	>	<	<	>	>>			
Transition time	<	<		>	<	<			

Note. **> refers to increase, < to decrease; double symbols indicate the predicted strength of the change; joint use of two symbols pointing in the opposite direction refer to cases where antecedent voice types exert influence in opposite direction**

derived from the basic predictions of the vocal responses to particular stimulus evaluation checks outcomes presented in Table 4.7. The expected acoustic consequences are listed in Table 4.9.

Given the fact that the predicted vocal responses for the various types of inappropriate affect are highly differentiated and, in many cases, pointing in different directions, it is obvious that the population of depressed patients to be studied needs to be subdivided in terms of the types of inappropriate emotion processes that are present. Because this has generally not been done in past studies, it is not surprising to find a lack of replication and many cases of overall trend reversals in the literature. There is a high likelihood that consistency in the results can be obtained if more homogeneous subgroups of patients, for whom the expected emotion-voice mechanism can be clearly specified, were to be studied. Similarly, at least for bipolar disorders, the specification of the phase in which the patient has been studied is of vital importance, because the underlying emotion processes (and the nature of the malfunctioning or inappropriateness) are clearly different in depressive and manic episodes—as are the vocal responses.

CONCLUSIONS

This has been a cursory overview of past research and possible new paradigms for the search for vocal indicators of affective disorders, particularly depression. As the review of the literature has shown, the field is beset by a large number of problems due to the difficulties of sampling patients, speech and voice utterances, and choosing the proper methodology for measurement. Yet, the theoretical considerations, as well as some of the more rigorously derived findings in the literature, assert the important role of vocal measurement as a central pillar in the behavioral measurement of affective disorder. There can be little doubt that the vocal musculature is a highly sensitive instrument likely to be strongly affected by changes in affective state. Furthermore, because the voice is a major medium for communication, the nature of the social relationships of the speaker is also likely to affect voice and speech processes.

Another fruitful approach to increasing our understanding of the relationships between affect, physiology, and voice production is the systematic study of the effect of psychoactive drugs on the voice. Preliminary studies (Helfrich, Standke & Scherer, 1984; Feldstein & Weingaertner, 1981) show that vocal analysis is a highly sensitive instrument to monitor the effect of various psychopharmacological agents. It is obvious that the combination of our knowledge concerning such psychophysiological and psychoneurological effects on voice production and of the changes due to clinically observable affect disturbances could greatly further our understanding of the processes underlying these effects.

Given the potential of the vocal measurement approach, it is surprising that so little use has been made of it to date. As has been mentioned in the introduction, one of the erroneous assumptions is that vocal information can be easily and intuitively gathered by clinicians that are practiced and highly skilled in interacting with and interviewing patients, even if these clinicians have not been specially trained for vocal analysis. A further hindrance for progress in this area has been the immense complexity of the vocal features and the technical difficulties and expense of measuring them. The latter problem is likely to be alleviated in the near future, at least as far as technology is concerned.

Although the analysis methods at the moment are still limited to research teams equipped with fairly sophisticated hardware and advanced computer facilities, it is likely that hardware and software that is within reach of the practicing clinician will soon become available. However, we have to avoid a situation in which the technological availability of such measurement procedures may outrun our understanding of the underlying psychological and physiological processes. Such understanding is definitely required for a sensible use of sophisticated vocal measurement. A frightening example of the potential dangers is provided by the pervasiveness of the so-called voice stress analyzers or voice-based "lie detectors" now available on the open market. Not only are there very serious doubts concerning the validity of the results produced by these devices, they are also frequently abused because of the users' ignorance about the basic requirements of such measurement and also because of the lack of solid research evidence concerning the relationships between specific acoustic parameters and stress or deception conditions.

REFERENCES

Askenfelt, G. & Sjölin, P. (1980). Voice analysis in depressed patients: Rate of change in fundamental frequency related to mental state. *Speech Transmission Laboratory - Quarterly Progress and Status Report,* Stockholm, 2–3, 71–84.

Bannister, M. L. (1972). *An instrumental and judgmental analysis of voice samples from psychiatrically hospitalized and nonhospitalized adolescents.* Unpublished doctoral thesis, University of Kansas.

Bildhauer, R. (1985). *Vokale Indikatoren depressiver Stimmung: Grundfrequenzänderung der Stimme depressiver Patienten und ihrer Interviewer in Abhängigkeit von der subjektiven Patientenbefindlichkeit.* (Vocal indicators of depressive mood.) Unpublished Diploma thesis, University of Giessen.

Beck, A. T. (1967). *Depression.* New York: Harper and Row.

Crystal, D. (1969). *Prosodic systems and intonation in English.* Cambridge: Cambridge University Press.

Crystal, D. (1975). *The English tone of voice.* London: Arnold.

Darby, J. K. (1981). Speech and voice studies in psychiatric populations. In J. K. Darby (Ed.), *Speech evaluation in psychiatry* (pp. 253–284), New York: Grune & Stratton.

Darby, J. K. & Hollien, H. (1977). Vocal and speech patterns of depressive patients. *Folia Phoniatrica, 29,* 279–291.

Darby, J. K., Simmons, N., & Berger, P. A. (1984). Speech and voice parameters in depression: a pilot study. *Journal of Communication Disorders, 17,* 75–85.

Denber, M. A. (1978). *Sound spectrum analysis of the mentally ill.* Unpublished master's thesis, University of Rochester.

Diamond, B. L. (1981). The relevance of voice in forensic psychiatric evaluations. In: J. K. Darby (Ed.), *Speech evaluation in psychiatry* (pp. 243–252), New York: Grune & Stratton.

Dittmann, A. T. (1972). *Interpersonal messages of emotion.* New York: Springer.

Eldred, S. H. & Price, D. B. (1958). The linguistic evaluation of feeling states in psychotherapy. *Psychiatry, 21,* 115–121.

Feldstein, S. & Weingaertner, H. (1981). Speech and psychopharmacology. In J. K. Darby (Ed.), *Speech evaluation in psychiatry* (pp. 379–396), New York: Grune & Stratton.

Fleischmann, G. (1980). *Akustisch-phonetische Untersuchungen an der Sprache der Depressiven (Acoustic–phonetic studies of depressive speech).* Unpublished master's thesis, University of Cologne.

Goldman-Eisler, F. (1968). *Psycholinguistics: Experiments in spontaneous speech.* New York: Academic Press.

Hargreaves, W. A., & Starkweather, J. A. (1964). Voice quality changes in depression. *Language and Speech, 7,* 84–88.

Hargreaves, W. A. & Starkweather, J. A. (1965). Vocal and verbal indicators of depression. Unpublished manuscript, San Francisco.

Hargreaves, W. A., Starkweather, J. A. & Blacker, K. H. (1965). Voice quality in depression. *Journal of Abnormal Psychology, 70,* 218–220.

Harlan, C. D. (1974). *Incidence and relationship of voice disorders within divergent psychotic populations.* Unpublished doctoral thesis, University of Utah.

Heitman, S. (1980). *Sprechstimmveränderungen bei Psychotikern: Untersuchung des Stimmspektrums bei depressiven, paranoid-halluzinatorischen und hebephrenen Schizophrenen über je 4 Interviews (Voice changes in psychotics: Studying the vocal spectrum in depressive, paranoid–hallucinatory, and hebephrenic patients across 4 interviews).* Unpublished doctoral thesis, University of Giessen.

Helfrich, H., Standke, R. & Scherer, K. R. (1984). Vocal indicators of psychoactive drug effects. *Speech Communication, 3,* 245–252.

Isserlin, M. (1925). Psychologisch-phonetische Untersuchungen. II. Mitteilung *(Psychological–phonetic studies: II. Note) Zeitschrift für die Gesamte Neurologie und Psychiatrie, 94,* 437–448.

Jürgens, U. (1974). On the elicitability of vocalisation from the cortical larynx area. *Brain Research, 81,* 564–566.

Jürgens, U. (1979). Vocalisation as an emotional indicator: A neuroethological study in the squirrel monkey. *Behaviour, 78,* 88–117.

Jimenez, A. (1981). El analisis de la voz en psicologia *(Vocal analysis in psychology).* Unpublished master's thesis, Autonoma University of Madrid.

Key, M. R. (1977). *Nonverbal communication: A research guide and bibliography.* Metuchen, NJ: Scarecrow Press.

Laver, J., & Hanson, R. (1981). Describing the normal voice. In J. Darby (Ed.), *Speech evaluation in psychiatry* (pp. 51–78), New York: Grune & Stratton.

Laver, J. & Hutcheson, S. (Eds.). (1972). *Communication in face to face interaction.* Harmondsworth England: Penguin.

Mahl, G. F. & Schulze, G. (1964). Psychological research in the extralinguistic area. In T. Sebeok, A. S. Hayes, & M. C. Bateson, (Eds.), *Approaches to semiotics* (pp. 51–124). The Hague: Mouton.

Moses, P. (1954). *The voice of neurosis.* New York: Grune & Stratton.

Newman, S. S. & Mather, V. G. (1938). Analysis of spoken language of patients with affective disorders. American Journal of Psychiatry, 94, 913–942.

Ostwald, P. F. (1961). The sound of emotional disturbance. *Archives of General Psychiatry, 5,* 587–592.

Ostwald, P. F. (1963). *Soundmaking: The acoustic communication of emotion*. Springfield, IL: C. C. Thomas.

Ostwald, P. F. (1964). Acoustic manifestations of emotional disturbance. *Disorders of Communication - Research Publications, 42*, 450–465.

Poyatos, F. (1976). *Man beyond words. Theory and methodology of nonverbal communication*. New York: The New York State English Council.

Robinson, W. P. (1972). *Language and social behavior*. Harmondsworth: Penguin.

Roessler, R. & Lester, J. (1976). Voice predicts affect during psychotherapy. *Journal of Nervous and Mental Disease, 3*, 166–176.

Scripture, E. W. (1921). A study of emotions by speech inscription. *Vox, 31*, 179–183.

Scripture, E. W. (1927). *Anwendung der graphischen Methode auf Sprache und Gesang (The use of the graphical method on voice and singing)*. Leipzig.

Scherer, K. R. (1981). Speech and emotional states. In J. K. Darby (Ed.), *Speech evaluation in psychiatry* (pp. 189–220). New York: Gruner & Stratton.

Scherer, K. R. (1982). Methods of research on vocal communication: Paradigms and parameters. In K. R. Scherer, P. Ekman (Eds.), *Handbook of methods in nonverbal behavior research* (pp. 136–198). Cambridge: Cambridge University Press.

Scherer, K. R. (1984). On the nature and function of emotion: A component process approach. In K. R. Scherer & P. Ekman (Eds.), *Approaches to emotion* (pp. 293–318). Hillsdale, N.J.: Lawrence Erlbaum Associates.

Scherer, K. R. (1986a). Vocal affect expression: A review and a model for future research. *Psychological Bulletin, 99*, 143–165.

Scherer, K. R. (1986b). Voice, stress, and emotion. In M. H. Appley, & R. Trumball (Eds.), *Dynamics of stress*. (pp. 159–181) New York: Plenum.

Scherer, K. R. *Towards a dynamic theory of emotion: The component process model of affective states*. Manuscript submitted for publication, University of Giessen.

Seligman, M. E. P. (1975). *Helplessness: On depression, development and death*. San Francisco: W. H. Freeman.

Tolkmitt, F. J., Helfrich, H., Standke, R., & Scherer, K. R. (1982). Vocal indicators of psychiatric treatment effects in depressives and schizophrenics. *Journal of Communication Disorders, 15*, 209–222.

Trager, G. L. (1958). Paralanguage: A first approximation. *Studies in Linguistics, 13*, 1–12.

Whitman, E. N. & Flicker, D. J. (1966). A potential new measurement of emotional state: A preliminary report. *Newark Beth-Israel Hospital, 17*, 167–172.

Zuberbier, E. (1957). Zur Schreib- und Sprechmotorik der Depressiven (On motor aspects of writing and speaking in depressive patients). *Zeitschrift für Psychotherapie und Medizinische Psychologie, 7*, 239–249.

Zwirner, E. (1930). Beitrag zur Sprache der Depressiven *(Contribution to the study of depressive speech). Journal für Psychologie und Neurologie, 41*, 43–49.

5 THE PACING OF SPEECH IN DEPRESSION

Aron W. Siegman
University of Maryland Baltimore County

This chapter deals with the temporal pacing of speech in depressed individuals and with the possibility that temporal indices of speech can serve as objective markers for major depressive disorder diagnoses. I will first review the research findings on the temporal pacing of speech in depression in a more or less chronological fashion, then proceed with a discussion of the mechanisms that may be involved in the obtained relationships, and conclude with guidelines for future research. Also the effects of depression on verbal productivity will be briefly reviewed.

EMPIRICAL FINDINGS ON THE EFFECTS OF DEPRESSION ON SPEECH RATE

Although it has long been recognized that motor retardation, including slow speech, is a major feature of clinical depression, careful empirical studies of the relationship between depression and the temporal pacing of speech are few and of fairly recent vintage. Moreover, in some studies the patients were not necessarily clinically depressed, that is, they did not qualify for a diagnosis of major depressive disorder according to DSM III. Nevertheless, they are included in this review to shed light on the relationship between depression and the temporal pacing of speech.

A study by Kanfer published in 1960 was perhaps the first to present objective empirical data on the relationship between depression and speech rate, although not all the participants of this study were necessarily clinically depressed. In this study, the participants (38 female psychiatric patients) responded to four general questions dealing with their living arrangements, family relations, sexual experiences, and their current illness. Verbal rate, or speech rate, was measured by number of words per 30-second periods. Individual Minnesota Multiphasic Personality Inventories (MMPIs), which were administered as part of the hospital testing routine, were available on all these patients. Of all the clinical scales in the MMPI, only the Depression scale correlated significantly and in the expected direction with the patients' speech rates ($-.333$, $p < .02$). Although the other two scales that comprise the so-called "neurotic triad," that is, the Hysteria and the Psychasthenia scales, as well as the Paranoia scale, also correlated negatively with the patients' speech rates, these correlations were not significant. These findings have been cited in the literature (Natale, 1977; Siegman, 1985) in support of the hypothesis that depression is associated with a relatively slow speech rate. In fact, however, the results of the Kanfer study are ambiguous. The ambiguity is a consequence of the fact that the significant negative correlation between the Depression scale and speech rate obtained only in one of the four topics, that is the patients' living arrangements (which was probably the least anxiety-arousing of the four questions for most of the patients). The interpretation and generalizability of these findings is further compromised by the fact that some form of schizophrenia was the primary diagnosis of most of the patients in the sample.

By way of contrast, the results of a study by Weintraub and Aronson (1967), who investigated the speech of depressed patients as part of a larger study on the speech style of psychiatric patients, are much more clear-cut. The subjects of the study were 45 hospitalized, clinically depressed patients—23 women and 22 men—and 46 controls divided equally between males and females. The participants were requested to speak for about 10 minutes about any subject that they wished to discuss. They spoke into a tape recorder in the presence of the experimenter, who remained in the background. The responses were analyzed for a number of stylistic variables including number of words spoken or productivity, long silent pauses, defined as silences of more than 5 seconds (the final score was determined by "adding all individual long pauses beyond the first five seconds"), and speech rate, defined as the total number of words divided by "the number of non silent minutes to the nearest 15 seconds." The depressed patients obtained significantly lower productivity scores, longer silences and slower speech rates than their counterparts in the control group.

Weintraub and Aronson's findings for *speech rate* were replicated by Hinchliffe, Lancashire, and Roberts (1970) with a group of 10 depressed patients and 10 matched controls. However, the *silence* data are reported differently in the two studies. Whereas Weintraub and Aronson report the total duration of the long pauses, Hinchliffe and her associates report their frequency and average duration. This difference makes it difficult to compare the two studies directly as far as the effects of depression on silence are concerned. Nevertheless, it would appear that Hinchliffe and her associates failed to replicate Weintraub and Aronson's findings for long silent pauses. In the Weintraub and Aronson study the patients obtained significantly longer pauses than the controls (195.8″ versus 82.4″), however, in the Hinchliffe et al. study the two groups did not differ significantly in relation to either the frequency or the average duration of their silent pauses. Given these discrepancies, it is surprising that the participants' speech rates were nearly the same in the two studies. Hinchliffe et al. did not present comparative data for productivity because they limited their participants to five minutes of speech.

In discussing their findings, Weintraub and Aronson (1967, p. 25) note that although most of their depressed patients spoke relatively little and slowly, some patients—whom they characterize as agitated depressives—showed the opposite pattern. Similarly, Hinchliffe et al. (1971, p. 472) report that three of their patients had fast speech rates. However, whether such variations represent random variability or systematic differences between retarded and agitated depressives can only be established on the basis of carefully planned comparisons between the two groups and not on the basis of post hoc speculations.

The validity of the Weintraub and Aronson (1967) and Hinchliffe et al. (1971) studies, which compared the verbal behavior of depressed and nondepressed individuals, depends on the appropriateness of the control group. Clearly, the two groups should be matched on *all* relevant variables, not just on age, sex, and a rough social-status index. It is not obvious, however, that such a complete matching was achieved in the Weintraub and Aronson study, in which hospitalized depressed patients were compared with Army volunteers and hospital employees. At the very least they did not control for hospitalization. Although the controls in the Hinchliffe et al. study were drawn from a surgical ward, there is no indication that they were matched with the depressed patients for length of hospitalization.

In a study by Pope, Blass, Siegman, and Raher (1970) the authors examined the effects of depression on speech in six hospitalized psychosomatic patients. Although not all of the patients had depression as their primary diagnosis, they all showed depressive symptoms during some period of their hospitalization. None showed psychotic symptoms. Each morning, for the entire period of their hospitalization, these patients talked into a tape recorder for about 10 minutes about their experiences during the previous day. A team of specially-trained nurses made daily ratings of each patient on a number of depression scales developed by Bunny and Hamburg (1963). The audio-recordings obtained from each patient during the 8 most-depressed days were compared with those made during the 8 least-depressed days, that is, the patients served as their own controls, on a number of speech indices. The speech indices included Silence Quotient, Speech Rate, and Articulation Rate. Silence Quotient was calculated by dividing all silent pauses 2 seconds and over by speaking time. Speech Rate was calculated in the usual way, that is, by dividing the total number of words by speaking time. Articulation Rate was determined by dividing the total number of words by speaking time, minus the silent pauses 2 seconds and over. It should be noted that the label "articulation rate" is really a misnomer because in calculating this index, the silences of less than 2 seconds were not removed from speaking time. In fact, this index is a combined measure of the speaker's articulation, or phonation, rate, plus the speaker's short pausing time (less than 2 seconds).

The expectation that the speech samples obtained during the high depression days would be associated with slower speech rates than would those obtained during the low-depression days was confirmed (1.03 versus 1.32 sec). The patients also obtained significantly higher Silence Quotient scores during the relatively depressed than during the relatively nondepressed days. However, there was no significant difference on the Articulation Rate index. This finding suggests that depression does not increase a speaker's articulation, or phonation, rate, because if it does it should have affected our participants' Articulation Rate scores, unless there was an unlikely negative correlation between depression and short silent pauses. In all likelihood, the significantly slower speech rates in the relatively depressed than in the relatively nondepressed days reflect differences in pausing time rather than differences in phonation time. It should be noted that the participants of this study were psychosomatic patients, not all of whom were necessarily clinically depressed. Thus, the absence of a relationship between depression and phonation rate in this group does not preclude such a relationship in a clinically depressed group, especially in patients with motor retardation. It should also be noted that in this study, unlike in previously cited studies, the participants were alone when they recorded their monologues. This setting is significant in that it rules out the possibility that the increase in long silent pauses and the resulting slow speech rate during the depressed days are merely a consequence of a lack of *social* responsiveness or a lack of concern with being interrupted by one's partner when one is depressed. Alternatively, the relatively long silent pauses and the resulting slow speech rate in depression can be a result of a lowered drive level and/or the intrusion of distracting depressed thoughts during periods of depression. If the latter is the case, then a relatively slow speech rate may be found in agitated as well as in retarded depressives.

One troubling aspect of the preceding study is that there was no control for topical focus. The patients may have discussed different topics during the depressed days than during the nondepressed days. The same problem plagues the studies by Weintraub and Aronson (1967) and Hinchliffe et al. (1971) in which depressed patients and control subjects were asked to talk about any topic that they wished from among a wide range of topics. The controls may have talked about topics different from those discussed by the depressed patients. Given the evidence that topical focus is a significant source of variance in speech rate, as well as in other temporal variables, this could be a serious confounding. The evidence clearly suggests that people speak more quickly, with shorter latencies, shorter silences, and more accelerated speech rates, when the topic of discussion is familiar rather than unfamiliar, and relatively neutral rather than anxiety-arousing (Siegman, in pressa). Also, neither the study by Pope et al. (1970), nor the previously cited studies, attempted to control for the effects of antidepressants or other drugs.

By way of summary then, it appears that although the studies reviewed thus far support the hypothesis that depression is associated with a decelerated speech rate (probably because of longer and/or more frequent silent pauses), there are sufficient ambiguities in the results of some studies and methodological shortcomings with others to require further evidence.

A study by Rutter (1977) focused on the patterning of speech in schizophrenic patients. It included three control groups: depressed patients, patients suffering from neurotic or personality disorders, and psychiatrically normal chest-pain patients. For the purposes of the present review, we compared the speech patterning of the depressed patients with that of the other two control groups—the neurotic-personality disorder group and the chest pain group. Each group consisted of 12 participants, 6 men and 6 women aged 18 to 60, and they were tested within 10 days of admission to the hospital, the majority within 6 days. Each participant took part in two five-minute discussions, one with a partner who was a patient from his/her own category, and one with a psychiatrically normal partner, who was generally a nurse. Each pair discussed an item modified from the Choice Dilemma Questionnaire (Kogan & Wallach, 1964) and tried to agree on a solution. Thus, Rutter's study differs from the others in that the speech samples involved conversations, rather than interviews or monologues, and that an attempt was made to control for topical focus. In both conditions, that is, whether the patients spoke to a fellow patient or to a normal partner, there were no systematic differences between the depressed patients and the others in relation to speech rate (Table 5.1). The authors also looked at several indices of productivity and at the frequency and duration of simultaneous speech (Table 5.1). The only significant difference involved duration of simultaneous speech in the patient-partner condition (Table 5.1), with the depressed patients spending significantly less time in simultaneous speech than the medical controls.

This, then, is the first and, to the best of my knowledge, the only study that has failed to find an association between depression and the temporal pacing of speech. It should be noted that the depressed patients in this study did not behave as depressed patients normally do in other respects as well. Elsewhere, Rutter (1976) reported the visual interactions of the same participants. In the normal-partner condition, the mean looking-time of the depressed patients was longer than that of neurotic-personality disorder group and that of the chest-pain group. Although the evidence is by no means unanimous in showing that depressed patients have significantly shorter looks than appropriate controls, to find the reverse is puzzling. As far as I can tell, there are no obvious methodological problems with the study that can account for the lack of significant findings as far as speech rate is concerned. There is, however, one difference between Rutter's

TABLE 5.1
Mean Speech Values of Depressed Patients and Control Groups in Rutter's (1976) Study

Speech Variables	*Patient Partner Condition*						*Normal Partner Condition*					
	Depressive		*N/P Disorder*		*Chest*		*Depressive*		*N/P Disorder*		*Chest*	
	Mean	*SD*	*Mean*	*SD*	*Mean*	*SD*	*Mean*	*SD*	*Mean*	*SD*	*Mean*	*SD*
% time spent speaking	53.6	15.1	41.4	19.8	49.8	20.5	50.8	19.2	49.6	20.7	58.1	10.2
Total no. words	439.6	123.4	372.8	186.0	416.3	166.9	436.6	196.6	431.8	150.3	472.4	111.2
No. utterances	18.5	6.5	16.5	7.8	19.8	8.1	14.7	4.6	18.7	5.9	18.2	6.7
Mean word length of utterance	26.1	12.9	32.9	40.7	21.2	9.3	29.5	12.8	27.5	20.0	27.8	11.0
Speech rate (words/sec)	2.7	0.6	3.0	0.6	2.8	0.6	2.8	0.5	3.0	0.5	2.7	0.4
% time spent in mutual silence	14.5	9.7	17.3	18.5	11.0	10.2	12.6	13.4	11.3	8.3	9.4	9.1
% time spent in simultaneous speech (SS)	5.3[a]	2.9	5.7	4.7	11.2[a]	5.5	5.1	2.7	5.4	3.6	7.4	3.8
No. occurrences SS	11.3	17.3	11.8	10.8	19.9	7.6	10.3	6.4	11.4	6.8	12.8	6.7
% occurrences SS initiated by subject	53.6	20.9	40.9	26.5	43.4	20.5	45.6	25.0	55.3	14.9	49.4	24.4
Filled pause ratio (% words)	2.4	2.2	1.9	1.5	2.6	1.8	2.5	2.4	2.6	1.5	2.9	2.0
Speech disturbance ratio (% words)	8.9	4.2	5.8	4.1	6.4	2.1	9.3	4.5	7.4	2.6	6.3	3.0

Note. Table adapted from Rutter (1976).
[a]The difference between the depressed and chest patients is significant ($t(20) = 3.29$, $p < .05$).

study and the others, and it involves the nature of the speaking task: a problem-solving task in Rutter's study and interviews and free speech in the others. It may very well be that this difference accounts for the discrepant findings—a possibility which will be discussed in greater detail later in this paper.

The next three studies to be reviewed all used a very simple speech task in order to assess the effect of depression on speech rate, namely, counting from 1 to 10 at one's desired rate. The first in this series of studies is by Szabadi, Bradshaw, and Besson (1976). The patients were four females each diagnosed as suffering from moderate depression, which, however, warranted hospitalization. None of the patients were on medication before admission, and they were not given any during the first two days after admission. During this period, they made their first two baseline speech recordings by counting from 1 to 10. Drug treatment (amitriptyline) started on the third day. Subsequent speech samples were obtained at weekly intervals, always at the same time of day. The final speech assessments occurred after recovery, on an outpatient basis. A control group consisting of four young adults (1 female and 3 males) made similar weekly recordings for a period of two months. Using oscilloscope tracings, the investigators photographed the voice tracings, which allowed them to make careful measurements, in milliseconds, of the speaker's phonation time and pause time. Both the phonation times and the pause times that were obtained in the control group were remarkably stable, with the final readings being very similar to the initial readings. In the patient group, however, the pause times tapered off systematically, with the pause times during the treatment phase being substantially lower than the initial, or baseline, pause times, and the pause times during the recovery period being lower than those of the treatment period. Although, for the group as a whole, the patients' initial or baseline pause times were higher than those of the controls, at least one patient had initial readings that were not much different from those of the controls. In contrast to pause time, the patients' initial phonation times were not much different from that of the controls, and they did not change as a function of treatment and recovery. The patients' pause time scores correlated highly with their depressive symptomatology, as measured by the Hamilton Depression Rating Scale (Hamilton, 1960), more so than with their Hamilton Retardation scores, or with their scores on a tapping test. Nurses' motility ratings did not yield any consistent information. In a follow-up, or validation study, Greden and Carroll (1980) administered the same speech task to seven endogenomorphic depressed patients—4 with unipolar (UP) and 3 with bipolar (BP) depression—and 2 controls. Like Szabadi et al. (1976), they too found a decrease in the patients' pause time from the pretreatment to the treatment to the discharge phase. (In the Greden and Carroll study, the final speech samples were obtained from the patients after their physicians had determined that they had entered a euthmic stage, but before hospital discharge). The mean pause time decrease was 43% for BP and 35% for UP depressives, with a range of 15% to 67%. In contrast to the patients, the two control subjects had only nominal reductions (5 and 12%). Furthermore, whether the patients were agitated (four out of the seven were) or not, and whether they were treated with tryciclics or with electroshock, the results were the same. As was the case in the earlier study, the patients' pause scores corresponded well with their Hamilton Depression Scale scores. By way of contrast, there was no correlation between the patients' Hamilton Depression scores and their scores on the retardation item of that scale, apparently due to the low retardation scores obtained by the agitated depressives. The only discrepancy with the Szabadi et al. findings concerns the phonation times, which were substantially reduced as a function of recovery in three of the four patients.

A second follow-up study by Greden, Albala, Smokler, and associates (1981) included 24 UP and 12 PB patients with endogenous depression and a control group of 19 nondepressed patients. (Eight control patients had a diagnosis of schizophrenia, 3 dementia, 2 phobic disorder, 3 other psychiatric disorders, 1 Briquet's syndrome and 2 had no psychiatric disturbance. The controls were younger than the depressed patients and were about equally divided between males and females, whereas the sex ratio in the depressed patients was 11:25.) As in the previous two studies the depressed patients' pause time became shorter during the course of hospitalization—by 49% in the UP and by 31% in the BP depressives, with little change (4%) in the controls. When baseline pause times among the three groups were compared statistically, UP depressives differed significantly from the controls ($p < .01$), PB depressives only marginally ($p < .09$). UP depressives could not be distinguished from the BP depressives using the baseline data. There were no significant differences between the three groups on discharge. It should be noted that while all the BP depressives showed a decrease in pause time from baseline to discharge, 3 patients out of the 24 in the UP group increased their pause time. Finally, there was no significant correlation between the patients' pause time measures and the subjective assessment of their psychomotor functioning as indexed by the motor retardation item of the Hamilton Depression Rating Scale.

Taken together, these three studies provide impressive support for the hypothesis that depression is associated with a slowing down of speech, and that this effect can be measured by a simple counting task, Moreover, they suggest that this effect occurs in both UP and BP depressives, and apparently even in agitated depressives, although this needs more systematic study. On the other hand, given the considerable individual differences in relation to pausing time, it is unlikely that this variable can be used reliably for differential diagnoses. Its primary use would seem to be for objectively monitoring changes in patients' level of depression.

One very recent study to look at the temporal pacing of speech of clinically depressed patients was conducted by Breznitz and Sherman (1987). The study is part of the NIMH Childrearing Study, of which Marian Radke-Yarrow is principal investigator. The study by Breznitz and Sherman (1987) focused on the verbal interactions of 14 depressed (unipolar depression) and 18 control mothers with their children on three separate occasions: while preparing lunch, during lunch, and while waiting for a medical examination. The latter was intended to produce a mildly stressful situation. It was initiated by entry of a "doctor" (a white-coated male experimenter) who explained that he would be performing an anthropomorphic examination of the child. He asked the mother to remove the child's shirt, shoes, and socks while he was setting up in the side room. Five-minute segments of each of these three interactions were analyzed by means of the Automatic Vocal Transaction Analyzer, or AVTA (Jaffe & Feldstein, 1970), a specialized computer system for measuring vocal time patterns. The data have not yet been fully analyzed, but it is already clear that these unipolar depressed mothers spoke with slower speech rates than the control mothers, on two of the three occasions,—the two involving lunch.[1] There was an analogous difference in relation to response latency, but this difference was only of borderline significance. On these two occasions, the depressed mothers also spent significantly less time talking to their children than the controls.

Interestingly, the depressed mothers were significantly more productive during the presumably stressful interaction (i.e., while waiting for a medical examination), than on the other two occasions. No such increase in productivity occurred for the control mothers. In fact, during the presumably stressful interaction, the depressed mothers were significantly *more* productive than the control mothers. Elsewhere it has been shown that moderate levels of stress and anxiety arousal are associated with an increase in productivity and speech rate and with relatively brief response latencies (Siegman, 1985; in press a). This may account for the finding that the speech correlates of depression during the nonstressful interactions were either washed out or reversed during the presumably stressful interaction. Also, from the productivity data, it would appear that waiting for the medical examination was more stressful for the depressed mothers than for the controls, which, of course, is not surprising.

The last study to be discussed in this section was recently completed in our laboratory. The participants were candidates for coronary angiography, rather than hospitalized depressives. Some of these patients tend to be depressed—perhaps in reaction to their coronary problems—and we wanted to assess the effects of this depression on their speech style, in order to partial it out from the relationship of coronary occlusion and speech style. To that end, we administered the Beck Depression Inventory (Beck, 1967). Each patient was also administered an expanded version of Rosenman's Structured Interview, or SI (Rosenman, 1978), with one half of the interview administered in an accepting and supportive style, and the other half in a challenging and provocative style. The interview was followed by an unstructured conversation. All of this verbal material was analyzed by AVTA, which yields a number of temporal indices includ-

[1]This finding was not reported in Breznitz and Sherman (1987).

ing: response latency, average duration of silent pauses (which includes all silent pauses 300 msec and over); the Proportionality Constant Ratio, which correlates very highly with number of words per sec, summed duration of vocalizations, or productivity; and two indices of simultaneous speech (those that result in a change of speaker turn, or interruptive simultaneous speech, and those that do not, or noninterruptive simultaneous speech). Hierarchical regression analyses, in which the patients' verbal indices were entered as independent variables and their Beck scores as the dependent variable, showed that the speech rate index accounted for 29% of the variance of the female patients' Beck scores. The high Beck scorers spoke more slowly than the low Beck scorers ($r(13) = -.59$, $p < .05$). But this was the case only for the female patients, and only in the nonchallenging interview. There was no such significant negative relationship between the depression scores and speech rate in the unstructured conversation or in the challenging and provocative interview. The only other significant finding was a *positive* relationship between the female patients' Beck scores and their productivity scores in the unstructured conversation ($r(13) = .50$, $p < .05$). These findings suggest two things: first, that the effect of depression on speech may be more pronounced in females than in males—implying that in investigating the relationship between depression and speech, we need to look separately at males and females—and second, that the effects of depression speech may not be invariant across situations. Interviews may yield different relationships than conversations, and nonstressful interviews may yield different relationships than stressful ones. The latter was also suggested by the Breznitz study, in which the inverse relationship between depression and productivity that occurred in relatively nonstressful interactions was reversed in the stressful one.[2]

DEPRESSION AND PRODUCTIVITY

Evidence consistently shows that depression is associated with a relatively slow speech rate—with only one study clearly failing to support this generalization (Rutter, 1977); however, the evidence is much less supportive of the assumption that depression is associated with a reduction in productivity.

Supporting the hypothesis that depression is associated with a decrease in productivity, are the studies by Weintraub and Aronson (1967) and Breznitz and Sherman (1987) although the results of the latter study indicate that, depending on the situation, depressed patients can also be *more* talkative than nondepressed controls. Negative results were obtained by Rutter (1977). In our study with angiographic patients, the correlations between patients' Beck and productivity

[2]Given these findings, perhaps it was no accident that the negative correlation between depression and speech rate reported by Kanfer (1960) obtained only when the interviewer focused on a nonanxiety-arousing topic.

scores were consistently *positive*, although not always significant. For the group as a whole, with sex covaried out, there was a near significant positive correlation between the patients' Beck and productivity scores in the nonchallenging interview ($r(40) = .304, p = .06$). For the females only, there was a significant positive relationship between Beck and productivity scores in the unstructured conversation ($p = .04$). As pointed out earlier, not all of these patients were clinically depressed. However, a study by Ellgring, Wagner, and Clarke (1980) suggests that even in clinically-depressed patients the relationship between the subjective experience of depression and productivity, or talkativeness, is far from being a strong one. Their subjects were five males and four females, aged between 33 and 57 years, and diagnosed as having an endogenous depression. Only those patients who had shown notable improvement in their state of well being during their hospitalization were selected for this study. They were interviewed and participated in a free conversation twice weekly during their hospitalization. A comparison of the initial (first three) and discharge (last three) video-taped interviews and conversations (5-minute segments of each) shows an increase in mean proportion of speech for six of the nine patients, but a t test for the increase in proportion of speech time for the group as a whole was not significant ($t(8) = 1.94, p > .10$). Further, three of the patients had higher initial speech time values than the mean speech time value at discharge for the group as a whole.

To conclude, while there is some evidence to suggest that depression is associated with a reduction in productivity, this relationship is not a very strong one, and depending on the situation, can be reversed. We need much more information about the specific circumstances that either enhance or attenuate this relationship.

DISCUSSION

While there is strong empirical evidence for the widely-held assumption that depression is associated with a reduction in speech rate (with positive results in nine out of ten studies)[3] it is not quite clear what accounts for this relationship. A

[3]There are at least two studies that used Velten's Mood Induction Procedure in order to experimentally determine the effect of depressed and elated moods on the pacing of speech. Natale (1977) found that the induction of a depressed mood was associated with an increase in silent pauses but not with a significant decrease in speech rate. By way of contrast, the elation induction had a significant effect on both of the above, as well as on other temporal indices—all in the expected direction. Brown (1985) found that the depression induction was associated with an increase in pause frequency, but had no significant effect on speech rate, while the elation manipulation had no significant effect on either of these two indices. It is quite possible, however, that the intervening tasks between the mood manipulation and the speech tasks, that were given to some of the participants of this study, weakened the effects of the mood manipulations. It is not at all clear, then, that relatively transient mood changes have the same effects on speech as clinical, or subclinical, depression.

slow speech rate can be a function of a prolonged phonation, or articulation, rate, and/or frequent short pauses, and/or an increase in the duration of the pauses. In order to determine which of these parameters is responsible for the inverse relationship between depression and speech rate, one should, ideally, conduct a study that includes measures of all the relevant parameters. In the absence of such a study, we have to rely on the process of elimination. The studies conducted by Szabadi et al. (1976) and by Greden and Carroll (1980) included indices of both phonation—or articulation—and pausing time. Depression had no effect on the depressed patients' phonation time in the study by Szabadi et al., and only on some of the patients' phonation time in the Greden and Carroll study.[4] The failure to find a stronger relationship between depression and phonation rate in these studies may be a function of the fact that the speech task in these studies involved counting from 1 to 10, which is highly automatic speech, rather than a more creative speech task. However, in the study by Pope et al. (1970), in which the participants discussed their experiences during the previous day, the evidence also suggests that their relatively slow speech rate during their depressed days was not a function of a slow phonation, or articulation rate. It remains to be determined whether the slow speech rate that we see in depression is a function of an increase in the *frequency* of silent pauses, or in the *duration* of silent pauses, or in both. The early studies are not of much help in this respect, even if they include measures of the frequency and the duration of silent pauses (e.g., Hinchliffe, Lancashire, & Roberts, 1971), simply because their criterion for a silent pause, namely, five seconds and longer, is much too high. There are only few pauses which exceed this criterion level, at least in interviews and conversations. In the Breznitz and Sherman study, which included indices of both the frequency and the duration of silent pauses 300 msec and over, depression increased the frequency but not the duration of the silent pauses. In our study with angiographic patients, at least as far as the female patients were concerned, depression affected both the frequency and the duration of their silent pauses about equally.

Clearly, we need more information about which of the various temporal parameters that contribute to a person's speech rate are affected by depression. Also, more information about the kind of silent pauses—short versus long—that are affected by depression, and even about their location in the patient's speech could be helpful in understanding what is responsible for the depressed patient's reduced speech rate. Our own work suggests that there is only a moderate correlation between indices of short and long pauses and that they probably serve

[4]Of course, it is possible that the measurements that have been used were not sufficiently sensitive to pick up the microchanges in phonation time. Kohnen (1986), at the University of Hamburg, using a measurement device which records speech activity in time intervals of 8 msecs, found changes in articulation rate as a function of alterations in mood states. Moreover, these changes in articulation rate could be measured before the alterations in mood state could be observed.

different psychological functions (Siegman, in pressa). Goldman-Eisler (1968) and Boomer (1978) have shown that the kind of information that is processed during silent pauses depends on their location in a person's speech, although the two investigators disagree on exactly what is being processed. Clearly, a more fine-grained analysis of the temporal patterning of speech in depression is essential before we can turn to the mechanisms that are involved in some of the findings.

There are, however, certain things that we can say with some confidence about the relationship between depression and a slow speech rate. Given the available data, we can rule out motor retardation as the only or even the primary cause of the depressed patient's slow speech rate. Suffice it to mention the failures to obtain significant correlations in depressed patients between speech rate and indices of motor retardation (Szabadi et al., 1976; Greden et al., 1981). Also since monologues are affected no less than dialogues, we can conclude that there is more to the depressed patient's slow speech rate than a simple lack of social involvement. One plausible alternative hypothesis is that the depressed patient's slow speech rate reflects a general reduction in energy level. Yet, there are two sets of findings that cast some doubt on this hypothesis as well. First, there are the findings which suggest that although depression is associated with a decelerated speech rate, it is not necessarily associated with reduced productivity. Second, if the slow speech rate is a result of a low energy level, it should also have a slowing effect on reaction time, or response latency. However, response latency was only marginally affected in the Breznitz and Sherman study and not at all in our study of angiographic patients. Obviously, these findings also argue against the motor retardation hypothesis. Similarly, the fact that the decelerating effect of depression on speech rate is not invariant across speech tasks also argues against the motor retardation hypothesis.

Yet another plausible alternative is that the depressed patient's slow speech rate is the result of the intrusion of negative and unpleasant associations—a hypothesis that may be difficult but by no means impossible to test. If intruding negative thoughts are indeed the cause for the depressed patient's slow speech rate, then conditions that maximize the probability of such intrusions should decrease the speech rate even further. Conversely, conditions that minimize the intrusion of negative thoughts should moderate or even reverse the decelerating effect of depression on speech rate. Earlier, the study by Rutter was cited (1977), which is the only study that failed to find an inverse relationship between depression and speech rate. Further examination of this study may be instructive as a hypothesis generating exercise. It will be recalled that unlike other studies in which patients are interviewed or asked to talk about themselves and their problems, in this study the patients engaged in a problem-solving task with a peer. This may be the kind of situation that minimizes the opportunities for intruding negative thoughts to occur, and hence the "normal" speech rate. Some students of expressive verbal behavior maintain that such behavior represents primary, unmediated correlates of emotion, uncontaminated by cognitive processes, not unlike physiological correlates of emotion (Zajonc, 1980). Elsewhere (Siegman, 1985), it has been shown that the evidence suggests that this is not the case. Whatever else is reflected by expressive behavior, it also reflects cultural norms, individual coping mechanisms and even impression management strategies. From this point of view, it should not be surprising that the relationship between depression and expressive behavior is more pronounced in some contexts (e.g., psychiatric interviews) than in others (e.g., problem-solving tasks). The demand characteristics of the psychiatric interview may encourage the expression of depressive feelings and behavior. The same perspective can also explain the apparent sex difference in the expressive correlates of depression, with some of the relationships between depression and speech apparently being more pronounced in females than in males. Elsewhere (Siegman, 1985), it has been suggested that the apparent sex differences in the expression of anger (with males expressing anger more freely than females) can be attributed to social norms that frown on the expression of anger in females. Perhaps the reverse holds true for the expression of depression. The expression of depressive thoughts and behavior may be more acceptable in females than in males and hence the apparent sex differences that were noted earlier in relation to speech rate in depressed patients.

THE ROLE OF EXPRESSIVE VOCAL BEHAVIOR IN THE MAINTENANCE OF DEPRESSION

Traditionally, students of depression have looked for the causes of depressed behavior *within* the patient, some focusing on psychological variables, others on biological factors. More recently, however, some students of depression have emphasized the role of social factors in maintaining depressed behavior. Depressive behavior may be initially maintained by the solicitous concern that it elicits from others, but eventually the patient's depressed affect and thoughts will drive others away and result in a loss of social support. This reduction in social responsiveness may initiate a vicious cycle, which will further reduce the depressed patient's social initiatives and skills, and hence the opportunities for social reinforcements (Coyne, 1976). It may very well be that the depressed patient's expressive behavior, especially the slow speech, the long response latencies, and the long silent pauses that have been discussed in this chapter play a significant role in this vicious cycle. Studies conducted in our laboratory and elsewhere have shown that expressive vocal behavior contributes significantly to interpersonal perception and attraction. By and large, people give unfavorable ratings and do not like others who speak exceedingly slowly, and with long silent pauses (for a summary of this research, see Siegman, in press a). It may very well be, then, that the depressed patient's slow speech and long silent pauses discussed in this chapter, and perhaps some of the other expressive vocal behaviors discussed in Chapter 4, contribute to the depressed patient's social isolation.

THE TYPE-A CONNECTION

Friedman and Rosenman (1974) have identified a set of behaviors, including competitiveness, job involvement, impatience, hostility, and time urgency, that put one at risk for coronary heart disease. Rosenman (1978) has developed a structured interview for the assessment of this behavior pattern. However, the assessment of Type-A behavior pattern is made not on the basis of content but rather on the basis of expressive style. Short response latencies, rapid accelerated speech, a loud voice, and frequent interruptions are some of the major stylistic variables that contribute significantly to a Type-A assessment. The converse of the Type-A expressive style, namely, a relatively slow speech rate, long response latencies, a soft voice, and few interruptions are the hallmarks of the Type-B individual. Given the findings on depressed patients reviewed in this chapter, it would seem that they speak like extreme Type-Bs. Unfortunately, none of the studies reviewed in this chapter include a systematic assessment of the speech stylistics of manic patients. However, if we can assume that the speech style of manics is the mirror image in the speech style of depressives, as is in fact suggested by clinical data, it would approximate that of extreme Type-As. If so, some individuals considered to be Type-As on the basis of their speech stylistics may in fact be manics, and conversely some individuals considered to be Type-Bs may in fact be depressives. Such confoundings may in fact be responsible for some of the recent failures to replicate the earlier obtained relationships between the Type-A behavior pattern and coronary heart disease (Siegman, in press; Siegman, Feldstein, Ringel, Tomasso, in press). One way to avoid such confoundings is to include measures of manic and depressive behavior in the assessment of the Type-A behavior pattern.[5]

In this connection, it is of interest to note the studies conducted in our laboratory and elsewhere on speech and cardiovascular reactivity. For example, Lynch and his associates (1985) reported a significant positive association between speech rate and cardiovascular reactivity, as indexed by blood pressure and heart rate. We found similar positive associations between loudness, interruptive speech, and cardiovascular reactivity (Siegman, Crump, Dembroski, &

[5]See Siegman (in press b) and Siegman et al. (in press) for other explanations for the recent failures to replicate the earlier finding of a positive association between interview derived global Type-A scores and coronary heart disease. One suggestion has been that the Type-A behavior pattern is a multidimensional construct only some of which are related to coronary heart disease, and of these hostility would seem to be the most plausible candidate.

Gjesdal, 1987; Siegman & Feldstein, 1985). Could it be that some of the speech and vocal correlates of depression-mania are mediated by SNS produced physiological changes that occur as a result of the affective disorders? Physiological measurements and pharmacological studies could be helpful in answering this question.

METHODOLOGICAL ISSUES

Much of the existing research on depression is seriously flawed from a methodological point of view. Although most of these methodological problems were introduced earlier, a more systematic review of these problems could be useful in guiding future research.

One obvious weakness of many previous studies is the restricted number of subjects. Studies in respectable journals are based on as few as four subjects. A failure to identify the patients' precise symptoms is yet another problem that is characteristic of many studies, especially the early ones. Many studies simply state that their patients were clinically depressed, without distinguishing between unipolar and bipolar depression, or agitated and retarded depressives. While Weintraub and Aronson (1967) and Hinchliffe et al. (1971) had the impression that the decelerating effect of depression on speech does not obtain in agitated depressives, data cited by Greden and Carroll (1981) suggest that this is not the case. Clearly, we need more information on this issue. Future studies should distinguish between these and perhaps between additional categories (e.g., endogenous versus exogenous) as well. Furthermore, with bipolars it is important to determine that they are not about to enter a manic cycle. Finally, there is a need for more information about manic patients, although their symptoms may make them difficult experimental subjects. Also, it is important to make separate analyses for males and females.

The selection of control subjects presents another difficult problem. Clearly, if the depressed group is hospitalized, so should the controls be. But from what patient group should they be selected? Some have used psychiatric patients such as schizophrenics and neurotics and personality disorders, but these groups too may have deviant speech patterns. A better alternative would seem to be medical patients, although with them too one can run into problems. For example, Rutter (1976, 1977) used patients with chest pain, many of whom must have been coronary patients whose speech pattern, as pointed out earlier, resembles that of manic patients. Perhaps the best alternative is to use depressed and manic patients as their own controls, and to monitor changes in their speech as their condition improves. In either case, whether one uses the patients as their own control or other patient control groups, it is important to control for the effects of antidepressants and other medications and treatments.

Yet another methodological problem is that of topical control. Some investigators simply give their subjects free rein to talk about anything they wish. However, depressed patients may select different topics for discussion than nondepressed ones. Similarly, depressed patients may talk about different topics depending on how depressed they feel. Because topical focus affects latency, speech rate, productivity, and other such variables (Siegman, in press a), this can be a serious source of error. Further, it is not sufficient to control the speech task, it should be systematically varied. Most studies investigating the effects of depression on speech rely on a single speech task, usually an interview. Yet the two studies that have varied the nature of the speech task (the Breznitz and Sherman study and ours with angiographic patients) found significant interactions with speech task. Therefore, in investigating the effects of depression on speech, one should look at its effects on dialogues as well as on monologues, on highly practiced, or "automatic" speech tasks as well as on spontaneous and creative speech tasks, on personal and impersonal topics as well as on problem-solving tasks. As has been shown earlier, differential effects as a function of speech task can provide insights about the mechanisms that mediate the relationship between depression and the temporal pacing of speech. Further, the use of different types of speech tasks may also be diagnostically useful. It should be of interest to know whether a patient's slow speech rate occurs only when the patient talks about his or her problems, or whether it occurs even when the patient talks about impersonal topics.

Finally, there is the issue of how to measure the temporal and other speech variables. Some investigators have used subjective judgments for determining interviewees' speech rate, loudness level and frequency of "overtalk" or simultaneous speech. However, results obtained in our laboratory indicate that the correlations between subjective estimates and objective measurements of response latency and speech rate are only moderate for the former (in the .40s at best) and not significant for the latter. The lack of a significant correlation between objective and subjective assessments of speech rate is a result of the fact that the subjective estimates of a speaker's speech rate are influenced by his loudness level. Conversely, estimates of loudness are influenced by speech rate (Bond & Feldstein, 1982). The correlations between subjective estimates and objective measurements of simultaneous speech are also only moderate (in the .40s). There are good grounds, then, for insisting on the objective measurements of these speech variables.

As has been pointed out earlier, if we wish to understand precisely what is involved in the relationship between depression and speech rate, we need fine-grained analyses of the patients' temporal pacing of speech. Studies that report on the amount of time spent in silent pausing but use 5 seconds as the criterion for a pause do not provide much useful information. Clearly, some of the measurements that are involved in such fine-grained analyses require sophisticated hardware, which is not widely available. However, as far as speech rate per se is concerned, a tape recorder and a stop watch will do.

PROSPECTUS

Despite the strong evidence that depression is associated with increased pausing times and slow speech rates, one must raise a note of caution about their use as *diagnostic* markers. The reason for this is the problem of individual differences. The pausing times and speech rates of depressed patients overlap to some extent with those of nondepressed individuals. Nevertheless, these indices could serve very well as objective markers of *changes* in depression. Significant decreases in pausing time and increase in speech rates occur with recovery, and they covary very strongly with patients' subjective ratings of depression. Furthermore, early decreases in pausing times are frequently predictive of ultimate clinical response to treatment (Greden & Carroll, 1980), a finding which has also been reported in relation to changes in eye contact (Ellgring et al., 1980). Although interesting, these findings about the predictive value of the temporal indices need to be replicated before they can be used as reliable predictors.

Although this review has focused on temporal variables, it is clear that for maximum value, future studies should monitor the effects of depression on the whole range of paralinguistic and nonverbal expressive behavior.

REFERENCES

Beck, A. T. (1967). *Depression: Clinical, experimental and theoretical aspects.* New York: Hoeber.

Bond, R. N., & Feldstein, S. (1982). Acoustical correlates of perception of speech rate: An experimental investigation. *Journal of Psycholinguistic Research, 11*, 539–557.

Boomer, D. S. (1970). A review of F. Goldman-Eisler, Psycholinguistics: Experiments on spontaneous speech. *Lingua, 25*, 152–164.

Breznitz, Z., & Sherman, T. (1987). Speech patterning of natural discourse of well and depressed mothers and their young children. *Child Development.*

Brown, J. F. (1985). The effect of induced mood on speech: Implications for the validity of the VMIP. Master's thesis, University of Maryland Baltimore County.

Bunny, W. E., & Hamburg, D. A. (1963). Methods for reliable longitudinal observation of behavior. *Archives of General Psychiatry, 9*, 280–294.

Coyne, J. C. (1976). Toward an interactional description of depression. *Psychiatry, 39*, 28–40.

Ellgring, H., Wagner, H., & Clarke, A. H. (1980). Psychopathological states and their effects on speech and gaze behavior. In H. Giles, W. P. Robinson, & P. M. Smith (Eds.), *Language: Social psychological perspectives.* Oxford: Pergamon Press.

Friedman, M., & Rosenman, R. (1974). *Type A behavior and your heart.* New York: Knopf.

Goldman-Eisler, F. (1968). *Psycholinguistics: Experiments in spontaneous speech.* New York: Academic Press.

Greden, J. F., & Carroll, B. J. (1980). Decrease in speech pause times with treatment of endogenous depression. *Biological Psychiatry, 15*, 575–587.

Greden, J. F., Albala, A. A., Smokler, I. A., Gardner, R., & Carroll, B. J. (1981). Speech time: A marker of psychomotor retardation among endogenous depressives. *Biological Psychiatry, 16*, 851–859.

Hamilton, M. (1960). A rating scale for depression. *Journal of Neurology, Neurosurgery and Psychiatry, 23*, 56.

Hinchliffe, M. K., Lancashire, M., & Roberts, F. J. (1971). Depression: Defense mechanisms in speech. *British Journal of Psychiatry, 118*, 471–472.

Jaffe, J., & Feldstein, S. (1970). *Rhythms of dialogue*. New York: Academic Press.

Kanfer, F. H. (1960). Verbal rate, eye blinks, and content in structured psychiatric interviews. *Journal of Abnormal and Social Psychology, 61*, 341–347.

Kogan, N., & Wallach, M. A. (1964). *Risk-taking: A study in cognition and personality*. New York: Holt, Rinehart & Winston.

Kohnen, R. (1986). *Validity of on-off patterns of speech in clinical psychology and psychopharmacology*. Unpublished manuscript, University of Hamburg, FRG.

Lynch, J. L. (1985). *The language of the heart*. New York: Basic Books.

Natale, M. (1977). Effects of induced elation-depression on speech in the initial interview. *Journal of Consulting and Clinical Psychology, 45*, 45–52.

Pope, B., Blass, T., Siegman, A. W., & Raher, J. (1970). Anxiety and depression in speech. *Journal of Consulting and Clinical Psychology, 35*, 128–133.

Rosenman, R. H. (1978). The interview method of assessment of the coronary prone behavior pattern. In T. Dembroski, S. Weiss, J. Shields, S. Haynes, & M. Feinleib (Eds.), *Coronary prone behavior*. New York: Springer-Verlag.

Rutter, D. R. (1976). Visual interaction in recently admitted and chronic long-stay schizophrenic patients. *British Journal of Social and Clinical Psychology, 15*, 295–303.

Rutter, D. R. (1977). Speech patterning in recently admitted and chronic long-stay schizophrenic patients. *British Journal of Social and Clinical Psychology, 16*, 47–55.

Siegman, A. W. (1979). Cognition and hesitation in speech. In A. W. Siegman & S. Feldstein (Eds.), *Of speech and time: Temporal patterns in interpersonal contexts*. Hillsdale, NJ: Lawrence Erlbaum Associates.

Siegman, A. W. (1985). Expressive correlates of affective states and traits. In A. W. Siegman & S. Feldstein (Eds.), *Multichannel integrations of nonverbal behavior*. Hillsdale, NJ: Lawrence Erlbaum Associates.

Siegman, A. W. (in press a). The telltale voice. In A. W. Siegman & S. Feldstein (Eds.), *Nonverbal behavior and communication* (2nd ed.). Hillsdale, NJ: Lawrence Erlbaum Associates.

Siegman, A. W. (in press b). In search of coronary-prone behavior. In R. Rieber (Ed.), *Man, communication and society. Essays in honor of Gregory Bateson*. Cambridge: Cambridge University Press.

Siegman, A. W., & Feldstein, S. (1985). The relationship of expressive vocal behavior and severity of coronary artery disease. Symposium paper presented at the annual meetings of the Society for Behavioral Medicine, New Orleans, LA.

Siegman, A. W., Feldstein, S., Ringel, N., & Tomasso, C. T. (in press). Expressive vocal behavior and the severity of coronary artery disease. *Psychosomatic Medicine*.

Siegman, A. W., Crump, D., Dembroski, T. M., & Djesdal, Gjesdal, J. (1987). Speech and cardiovascular reactivity. Paper presented at annual meetings of the Society for Behavioral Medicine, Washington, DC.

Szabadi, E., Bradshaw, C. M., & Besson, J. A. O. (1976). Elongation of pause time in speech: A simple, objective measure of motor retardation in depression. *British Journal of Psychiatry, 129*, 592–597.

Weintraub, W., & Aronson, H. (1967). The application of verbal behavior analysis to the study of psychological defense mechanisms. IV: Speech pattern associated with depressive behavior. *The Journal of Nervous and Mental Disease, 144*, 22–28.
Zajonc, R. B. (1980). Feeling and thinking: References need no inferences. *American Psychologist, 35*, 151–175.

Author Index

D

E

F

G

H

I

J

Subject Index